D1083661

4 ⁵⁰

"/2

THE KOEHLER METHOD OF OPEN OBEDIENCE
FOR RING, HOME AND FIELD

Also by William R. Koehler:

THE KOEHLER METHOD OF DOG TRAINING
THE KOEHLER METHOD OF GUARD DOG TRAINING
THE WONDERFUL WORLD OF DISNEY ANIMALS

The Koehler Method of

OPEN OBEDIENCE

for Ring, Home and Field

by William R. Koehler

Includes step-by-step retrieving with guaranteed results.

1980—Eleventh Printing

HOWELL BOOK HOUSE

230 PARK AVENUE

NEW YORK, N.Y. 10017

"Big Red", Irish Setter featured in the film of the same name, pictured with actors Emile Genest and Gillie Payant. "Big Red" was trained by the author.

Copyright © 1970 by Howell Book House Inc.
Library of Congress Catalog Card No. 70-114681
Printed in U.S.A.   ISBN 0-87605-753-9

No part of this book may be reproduced without permission in writing from the publisher.

Contents

ACKNOWLEDGMENTS

I wish to express my appreciation to Dick Koehler for assisting in the illustrating of this book, and to the individuals and organizations who have contributed so much to the success of our Open classes.

—*Bill Koehler*

Foreword

IF you aim to train your dog to retrieve—whether it be for the field, for the Obedience ring, or just for kicks—this is the book for you.

Conscientiously follow the instructions of this book and you will have a dog that will retrieve with absolute certainty, regardless of distractions.

Moreover, he will be trained to perform all the other requirements for the Open Obedience degree with this same total reliability.

Strong claims? Yes. But it is this proven ability to train dogs so that they perform with 100% reliability in the face of any distractions that has put the Koehler methods in the forefront of Obedience teaching today.

Each assignment is set at a level that experience has proven to be right. The dog is challenged with distractions at every level, and not until he has proven himself free of all contentions at one level, is he allowed to go on to the next.

Nowhere is this guarantee of perfect performance appreciated more than it is on the movie lots. With each day's filming costing thousands of dollars, the studios just cannot afford retake after retake. A flawless performance the first time out is a "must" for the movie dog. The achieving of such faultless performances, despite the thousand and one distractions on the set, stands as a tribute to the trainer, and his training methods.

Author William Koehler is chief dog trainer for the Walt Disney Studios, and one of the most respected in his field. Included in the honor roll of famous dogs he has trained are such award-winners as "Asta," "Wildfire," "Big Red" and "Boomerang". It is significant that the methods Mr. Koehler used to train these dogs for the movies are the same that he presents here for training your dogs.

Mr. Koehler has also had much experience in teaching owners to train their dogs. The affidavit that follows this Foreword, and the one that appears on Pages 46 and 47, attest to the many obedience and field training classes he has conducted.

This is the third book to feature the Koehler methods of dog training. The first, published just under a decade ago, was "The Koehler Method of Dog Training" and its impact was sensational. A guide for the beginner in Obedience, it has virtually revolutionized training methods throughout America. It continues to be one of the best selling of all dog books, and has been the primer for tens of thousands of novices.

The second, published in 1967, was "The Koehler Method of Guard Dog Training", and applied the Koehler concepts to the training of police and protection dogs. It was voted "Best Dog Book of the Year" by the Dog Writers' Association.

Now, this new book applies the Koehler methods to the more sophisticated requirements of the Open Obedience degree. We believe you will find it every bit as effective and serviceable as its predecessors.

One note. It is assumed that readers using this text will have already trained their dogs past the requirements for the Novice degree. If you are just a beginner, we suggest that you first graduate your dog past the exercises of "The Koehler Method of Dog Training" (Howell Book House).

—The Publishers

AFFIDAVIT

Burbank, California
May 12, 1967

TO WHOM IT MAY CONCERN:

I, Raymond E. Shultz, residing at 732 Screenland Drive, Burbank, California, do hereby certify that the following information, pertaining to the experience and accomplishments of W. R. Koehler, of 5059 State Street, Ontario, California, is factual.

According to War Department Credentials, Mr. Koehler served as a dog trainer at the Pomona Ordnance Base, and was transferred from that Base to the War Dog Reception and Training Center, San Carlos, California, where he served as a Principal Trainer. Further evidence establishes, that in addition to instructing officers and enlisted men, Mr. Koehler did training of a specialized nature.

From July 1946 through this date, Mr. Koehler has served as Chief Trainer for the obedience program of the Orange Empire Dog Club, the largest open membership dog club in the United States. Statistics show that during this period more than 14,000 dogs participated in the obedience classes sponsored by the above organization. He also conducted classes in tracking and specialized training for that club.

From 1946 through 1957 Mr. Koehler served as Class Instructor for obedience classes sponsored by the Boxer Club of Southern California. Club records show that during that period more than 1100 dogs participated in these classes.

Mr. Koehler served as Instructor for obedience classes sponsored by the Doberman Pinscher Club of Southern California. During the period of his instruction, 90 dogs participated in these classes.

From 1954 through 1960, Mr. Koehler served as Instructor for the Field Dog Classes sponsored by the Irish Setter Club of Southern California, which are open to all pointing breeds. Records show that 140 dogs have received instruction in this specialized training program.

Additional classes, for which the number of participants has been substantiated, bring the total number of dogs trained in Mr. Koehler's classes to well over 15,700.

The following innovations have been accredited to Mr. Koehler's work in the field of obedience classes:

Introduction of foundation work with a longe line, in conjunction with a complete absence of oral communication, as an emphatic means of instilling attentiveness into a dog.

Introduction of a system of gradually diminishing the length of a light line, used in conjunction with other equipment, as an assurance of a dog's reliable off-leash performance.

Development of more widely applicable methods of rehabilitating fighters, biters, and other major offenders. There is no record of his ever having refused a dog the opportunity for rehabilitation for any reason.

Establishing class procedure which demanded that all class participants make emphatic corrections, and which ruled out tentative, nagging corrections on the premise that an indefinite approach to animal handling constituted a major cruelty. Later this contention was supported with evidence supplied by an internationally accredited scientist who revealed that the use of electro-encephalograph equipment, of the same type used by the medical profession, showed that the training efforts of an indeterminate person cause great emotional disturbance to a dog.

Following are some of the accomplishments resulting from Mr. Koehler's efforts in the field of obedience classes:

The rehabilitation of an unsurpassed number of problem dogs, many of which were referred to his classes by humane organizations and law forces as a last hope to avoid destruction.

The generating of competitive obedience dogs, outstanding in numbers and quality even in the Los Angeles area, which, according to The American Kennel Club statistics, is by far the greatest obedience center in the United States.

A record of effectiveness and provision for the physical welfare of dogs that has caused his formats and training methods to be adopted by more obedience clubs than those of any other trainer in this region.

Three of the owner-handled dogs from his Field Classes have become Field Champions and many others have won points.

I have viewed letters from law forces in evidence of his personal experience in the areas of police work and tracking with dogs.

As an indication of the standard of performance exhibited by motion picture dogs he has trained, four of the number have been selected as deserving of the Achievement Award by the American Humane Association. "Wildfire" received the award for his performance in the picture "It's a Dog's Life," presented for the outstanding animal actor in 1955. The honor went to "Chiffon" for his performance in the picture "The Shaggy Dog" in 1959. "Asta," trained by Mr. Koehler and handled by him and his associate, Hal Driscoll, received the award for best television performance by an animal because of his work in the series, "The Thin Man." "Big Red," trained by Mr. Koehler, received the award for 1962.

My qualifications for the aforementioned statements are as follows:

1. Obedience Chairman—Boxer Club of Southern California, Inc. (5 years).
2. President—Boxer Club of Southern California, Inc. (1 year).
3. Delegate to the Southern California Obedience Council (5 years).
4. President—Southern California Obedience Council (2 years).
5. Vice President—Hollywood Dog Obedience Club, Inc. (2 years).
6. President—Hollywood Dog Obedience Club, Inc. (2 years).
7. Chairman of an Advisory Committee to the Southern California Obedience Council (2 years).
8. Director—German Shorthaired Pointer Club of Southern California (1 year).
9. Presently serving as President of the German Shorthaired Pointer Club of Southern California.

Raymond E. Shultz

Raymond E. Shultz

Subscribed and sworn to before me this _12th_ day of _May_, 1967.

Dorothy T. Hoffman

DOROTHY T. HOFFMAN

My Commission Expires November 3, 1969

DOROTHY T. HOFFMAN
NOTARY PUBLIC - CALIFORNIA
PRINCIPAL OFFICE IN
LOS ANGELES COUNTY

"Boomerang", star of the Walt Disney T.V. film, "Boomerang, Dog of Many Talents" counts his turkeys. Trained by the author.

To the memory of
Glen R. Beattie

"Boomerang" does a sit-stay on the bouncing seat of a wagon.

1

Basic Retrieving

IT is widely known that dependability in retrieving is required of the dog used in certain areas of the hunting field, in other vocations and in advanced obedience competition. Regrettably, few dog owners know how the retrieving exercise, if soundly motivated, can be used to instill confidence in a timid dog, develop other desirable qualities of character and generally improve his relationship with his master.

The affidavits in the front part of this book reflect experience in most vocations where dogs work at retrieving. Review them carefully. They will help you accept the conditions whereby you can successfully use the instructions presented for training your dog to retrieve. These conditions are:

(1) You must recognize that the positive motivations explained herein are completely dissimilar and opposed to the "make-a-game, play-ball, get the nice stick" method by which the uninformed cajole, rehearse and "hope" a dog toward uncertain retrieves that will be made only if the moment offers no more appealing "game" for the dog to play.

(2) You must proceed without deviating from the method in its philosophy, mechanics, sequence or time intervals.

Observe the two conditions. You will soon understand why the method is superior to the "play-ball, make-a-game" variety of retrieving for the obedience ring and for work.

Do not worry that force retrieving will be hard on your dog. You can employ a principle in such a way as to train him to retrieve reliably with even less discomfort than he experienced when you taught him to heel. And what does the dog think of the requirement that he retrieve whatever and whenever his master wishes? There is a ready answer to that question.

For many years the classes of the Orange Empire Dog Club have been among the larger facilities in the dog world for the teaching of reliable retrieving for the field and obedience ring; consequently, surveys conducted through the participants in this program should carry conviction to those who would romp to reliability by "making a game."

These surveys showed that by the seventh lesson all persons training in these classes had observed demonstrations of reliability which they agreed could not be matched by the coaxing, "game-type" retrieving. Another fact established is that the dogs which had never played any kind of a retrieving game learned as fast and performed as happily as the most "ball-happy" members of the numbers surveyed.

These findings reflect the accomplishments of average dogs that are trained in classes by owners of varying ability. They show that your reasonable effort will achieve complete success, and that the method used must indeed be effective.

To protect all concerned against the thoughtless person who would be so foolish as to start retrieving work with a dog that isn't well-grounded in the novice exercises, I would like to emphasize that a "test of readiness" is especially important to retrieving. When your dog will perform all of the novice obedience exercises acceptably, he'll be solid on his STAY positions and you'll be able to focus him properly.

Equipment

Start with a dumbbell of the type and size that your dog would require in the obedience ring, even though your dog may be used in the hunting field or some other kind of retrieving. The following will describe what the American Kennel Club has approved. (Obedience Regulations, Chapter 2, Section 17).

". . . *Shall be made of one or more pieces of one of the heavy hardwoods, which shall not be hollowed out." "The size of the dumbbell shall be proportionate to the size of the dog."*

The right kind of dumbbells are advertised in dog magazines and displayed in the better pet shops. There is no valid reason to believe that retrieving a dumbbell will make a dog hard-mouthed on birds. In fact, the opposite may be true. Later, you can switch to other training objects, including a variety of bundles and dummies, providing the dog is force-broken to retrieve. You'll find these discussed on page 141.

Level 1—Objective: acceptance of the dumbbell on command

Work your dog on the novice obedience exercises until he is at the peak of attentiveness. Stop, and when he sits beside you, give him a STAY command, and remain standing beside him. Drop the leash so that you can stand on it at a midway point. This is to make certain that should your dog become confused, and move while you are occupied with the dumbbell, you will not goof up a good beginning by fumbling for the leash to make a STAY correction.

Now let everything in your attitude and actions combine to give your dog a most dignified and pleasant introduction to the dumbbell. Certainly smearing meat on the dumbbell or using lilting, coaxing tones would offend the dignity of any dog who has had novice training.

Place your left hand across the dog's muzzle midway between the nose and eye with the thumb toward you and your fingers on the far side as you see illustrated on page 19. With the dumbbell centered in the palm of your right hand, bring

17

it against the dog's mouth as shown. Give a command: "Joe, fetch!", tightening your fingers and thumb against his lips to open his mouth just as though you were giving a pill and roll the dumbbell onto the lower jaw. As the dumbbell leaves the right hand, your thumb and fingers close gently on the end of the muzzle so that the mouth can be held shut for a few seconds while the left hand moves from its "opening position" back to scratch the dog's head around the root of the ear or wherever he seems to enjoy it. Add a bit of praise to the scratching. Next, move your right hand from his muzzle to the dumbbell, say, "Joe, give," and take it gently from him. Give him a word or two of praise for releasing the dumbbell.

To finish the exercise, move him from the STAY and give him an "Okay" release.

Consider this exercise from the dog's viewpoint. His mouth was opened gently. The strange word "fetch" was spoken as a pleasant association with the action. While the dumbbell was not particularly inviting, it was not discomforting. It was only in his mouth a few seconds, and the scratching and praise showed you were highly pleased with the situation.

In association with the word "give" you took the dumbbell from him before the first experience could become distasteful. The procedure was like asking a person to hold a piece of wood in his mouth while you stuffed ten-dollar bills into his pocket.

Repeat the above process a total of ten times during two or more training periods the first day, being calm and careful in your handling, and consistent in your effort to make each experience a pleasant association with the words of command.

The foregoing is typical of the first experience with at least 95% of the trainers who use the above procedure. A very small percentage of dogs have a built-in resistance to new situations, although the hang-up is generally erased if the fundamental obedience is thorough. Such a dog might attempt to jerk away from the hand that opens his mouth, move completely from position or go through a routine of contortions designed to keep the "new thing" from his mouth.

18

A foot secures the leash during the dog's pleasant introduction to the dumbbell.

The above training situation is set up so that the handler of the "exceptional" dog has an ace up his sleeve. *Remember —the dog was placed on a STAY, and it's a rare dog that can offer all-out resistance and concentrate on the responsibility of holding his STAY at the same time. If he moves, you are perfectly justified in correcting him with such force that he'll do more concentrating than resisting.*

With such a character, a lot more is lost than can be gained by coaxing him to accept an action that is reasonable to 95% of the dogs.

When he sees that he does not dare break the STAY, you'll be able to put enough pressure on his lips to open his mouth to the dumbbell. Be firm but calm, so that the introduction of the dumbbell does not suggest punishment. Complete the exercise just as you would when handling a normal dog. After a few experiences, the dog will be resigned to the fact that he might as well be as cheerful as you are about the situation.

More troublesome than the "resisters" are the chase-happy dogs whose buoyancy makes them want to grab anything that's held before them, together with the curious dogs who want to mouth strange objects. Their willingness is not much of a problem but their trainers generally are. They wail, "But why do I want to place the dumbbell in my dog's mouth when he is so eager to take it?" There is a reason—a very good reason.

For you to place that dumbbell in the dog's mouth one time when *you* "want to" brings us closer to our final objectives than if the dog grabbed it a hundred times because he "wants to." *Too often a poor handler, against all advice, will permit his eager dog to lunge out and grab the dumbbell instead of holding the dog to a controlled pattern in association with a command.* The price of such a mistake is high. Regardless of your dog's attitude and previous experience in retrieving, you will gain much and lose nothing by following step-by-step the formula of this book.

In technique, your work on the second day is exactly the same as it was on the introduction. Use at least two training periods, separated by as many hours as you find convenient, to give your dog at least two dozen experiences with the dumb-bell, which can be interspersed with other exercises and short breaks. By the end of the second period your dog will adapt a relaxed attitude toward this "thing of the dumbbell" and the words associated with it. Be certain your handling and the timing of the words are consistent so that the association will be strengthened.

Regardless of the dog's cooperation or other favorable signs, continue to work the dog daily, without changing the established pattern, for the next five days. Resist the temptation to change even if your dog is starting to respond by opening his mouth to the dumbbell before the pressure is applied to his lips. In fairness to yourself and the dog don't test his initiative yet.

This precept of practicing a dog extensively at each level, insuring comprehension in a way that makes failure highly improbable before entrusting response to his initiative, is one that we'll use all through this course in retrieving.

It's been seven days since you started work on retrieving, and the objectives of the first lesson should have been reached: your dog should understand the meaning of the words "fetch" and "give" in association with the dumbbell. Now it will be D-day for either you or the dog: either you will be unyielding on the first of a progression of reasonable demands or your dog will decide he can make you compromise right from the start and will best you at every turn.

Take your position with the dog on the SIT-STAY beside you. Snug the collar up close and as high on his neck as possible and hold the running part with your left hand exactly as is shown on page 22. Hold the dumbbell with your right hand by an end and place its shaft against the dog's mouth. Command, "Joe, fetch!" and press the dumbbell against his lips until he opens his mouth. Hold the dumbbell in his mouth for a couple of seconds, no more, while you praise him. Then tell him, "Give," and take it from him. Top it off with an extra bit of praise and move him from the spot.

Have the collar high and snug.

Problem? You say: "It won't slide into his mouth because he locked his jaws." Think for a bit, and you won't go back to helping him open his mouth. You opened it for seven days. That was plenty of time for him to learn what you want. Now you must make the first of your absolute stands. With the collar held rigidly, bring the dumbbell to bear against his mouth as you say, "Joe, fetch!" Keep that pressure there, regardless of how he turns his head, until he opens his mouth as he knows he should. Whether you gold-bricked in your training, or the dog is the rare exception that actually has difficulty in understanding this simple obligation, don't turn back now. *With no coaxing or impatience, keep going.* It may be that the relentless dumbbell will have to ride his lips for fifteen or twenty minutes before he realizes that you are not going to give up.

Don't let any theorist tell you that your dog will get an inhibition from this pressure. A dog that refuses the dumbbell after seven days of the association described above does so from cussedness and his trainer's lack of will power, not from stupidity and inhibitions. Win this test of wills; then praise the dog so warmly that he'll feel his decision to open his mouth was a profitable one.

For your encouragement and assurance I will tell you why I make such positive statements on how a dog will respond to the dumbbell. The previously mentioned surveys have shown how much time in the class format should be allotted to each level of training. A fact established is that only one dog in thirty would refuse to open his mouth willingly to the dumbbell after a week of the training described in the preceding lesson. Obviously there is no contradiction between the effort to make the introduction to the dumbbell as pleasant as possible and achieving the week's objective even if the dog's obstinacy causes his discomfort. At the start, the dog didn't understand the significance of the words and the dumbbell, and the pleasant association was needed to make him receptive to what you were teaching. By the end of the week he knows bloody well what you want, and for him to stymie you would do great harm to your cause.

You now have all the instruction and incentive needed to bring your dog to a level where he willingly opens his mouth to the touch of the dumbbell by the eighth day of work.

Whether your dog is one of the majority who readily opened his mouth to the pressure of the dumbbell or one of the rare ones who resisted it, give him a few more opportunities, then leave the exercise for the day.

Work him that same number of times for each of the next two days—more if needed—so that his performance and your praise will take him to a point where he opened his mouth cheerfully at the first touch of the dumbbell. Then you'll have the foundation for the next lesson.

Level 2: Objective: To reach one inch for the dumbbell

You will be helped abundantly by giving thought to the sequence of motivations used at previous levels before you begin this lesson. First there was enough finger pressure on your dog's lips to cause him to open his mouth, together with the praise that made the experience pleasant. A week of that association motivated him to open his mouth voluntarily when the dumbbell was pressed to his lips. Then came two more days of practice to strengthen that motivation. With the continuity of the above steps in mind, you are ready to familiarize yourself with the mechanics of the next motivation.

Place your dog beside you on a SIT-STAY close to a creature or object which you believe would be a distraction to your dog. Put your dumbbell in a pocket or inside your shirt so that you'll have both hands free for a few moments. Snug the collar up firmly and so high on the neck that your left thumb will be by the dog's ear. Use your right hand to arrange the ear between the running part of the collar and the thumb. When the collar is in the correct position, there is no dog too small to permit the use of this grip. With his foundation of obedience training, the dog will probably take the snugness of the collar as a further cue to stay; but if he tries to move, be careful to stop him without increasing the thumb

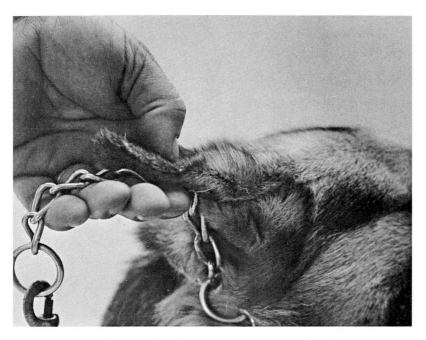

The collar and thumb pressure does not twist the ear.

pressure. It is essential that such discomfort come only when justified.

Watch your dog carefully. At a moment when he appears occupied with the distraction, place the dumbbell lightly—no pressing—against his mouth and give the command to fetch. If he responds in the presence of the distraction, cage his jaws gently with your right hand for a few moments of praise, then tell him to "Give," and take the dumbbell. His performance when exposed to distraction reflects your training.

It is now and at subsequent points of distraction that the "natural retriever" fails to retrieve naturally.

If he does not immediately respond to your command to take the dumbbell, press down on the ear with your thumbnail with enough force to make him open his mouth from surprise and discomfort. *Do not pull or twist the ear.* As the mouth opens, use your grip on the collar to move his head forward so that his jaws will encompass the dumbbell.

Do not move the dumbbell into his mouth—move his mouth over the dumbbell.

The instant the dumbbell is in his mouth, take your thumb from his ear and proceed to praise him. Then finish the exercise in the manner prescribed above.

Failure to take the thumb pressure from the dog's ear the instant the dumbbell enters his mouth will cause him to be corrected in association with what you want him to do, resulting in cruel confusion.

So that you will act with the positive attitude necessary to dog training, let's take a look at that last experience from the dog's point of view. The many times that he opened his mouth voluntarily in association with the touch of the dumbbell and the word "fetch" is proof that he understood your command. The fact that the touch of the dumbbell was very light and a distraction was present did not lessen his understanding nor his responsibility to perform. If he responded promptly to your command, he received praise. If he failed to respond, he got a correction that was the acme of logic. The instant he received the discomfort for disobeying a command that he fully understood, his head was shoved forward, which pressed his lips against the dumbbell with that familiar association, adding its meaning to the ear pressure and precluding any possibility of his misunderstanding. He felt relief the instant the dumbbell was in his mouth. His conclusions were fortified by your praise. Even the one experience may have begun to make him aware of another fact: it's better to move the mouth to the dumbbell than to wait for the dumbbell to move toward the mouth.

Add to his feeling of success by following up with a few exercises that he enjoys. Then repeat the pattern exactly as it is described.

Regardless of how willing your dog appears to be, continue to have the thumb and ear arrangement in the ready position. *Fumbling your way into a correction if the dog fails to respond can wipe out the gains you've made. Failure to get the pressure off his ear when he responds properly can be even more harmful.*

During your first period at this level of training, work on the retrieve pattern, interspersed with other exercises, until your dog has moved his mouth over the dumbbell five times without receiving pressure on his ear. Probably your dog will do that number without a single incident of contention. But if he's one of the rare ones who would test you at this level, persevere until he's been praised for the five contention-free experiences, which need not be consecutive.

Lest any screams of protest from either the dog or a nearby "wincer" embarrass you, consider this: our surveys show that there are apparently no dogs with the proper foundation who fail to comprehend what is wanted of them at this level. Work in the seculsion of the basement or the boondocks if you must, but don't let the *commiserados* weaken your reasonable demands.

Your work on the following day should be identical to that prescribed above. *Don't let his improved performance tempt you to give a command when the thumb and ear are not in the ready position. Don't fail to relieve the pressure at the right instant.* Increase the required contention-free experiences from five to ten.

You may be concerned over the fact that your dog passes his jaws loosely over the dumbbell but makes no effort to close his mouth. *Relax. We'll discuss the HOLD at the right time.* Work your dog for as many training periods as are necessary to bring him to the point where he consistently moves his jaws over the dumbbell without waiting for your thumb pressure.

By this time it has occurred to you that in order to move his jaws forward to accommodate the dumbbell, your dog has been actually reaching. You're right. It is now reasonable for you to start extending that reach, providing you follow a definite pattern.

Start the period by giving him two opportunities to respond willingly with the dumbbell held lightly to his lips in the familiar way. While he's still affected by the praise from these successes, set up the same kind of pattern in the same place. *This time, instead of holding the dumbbell against his lips, hold it about an inch from them.*

If he reaches on your command, cage his jaws long enough for the praise, and take the dumbbell. If he fails to respond to command, use the ear pressure to open his mouth and the snug collar to move it forward.

Move his mouth—not the dumbbell.

During the first period of training on the one-inch reach continue to work methodically and steadily until your dog has responded to command five times without need of correction. The five successes need not be consecutive.

There is a good reason why you should work methodically and steadily on the short reaches instead of interspersing the patterns with other exercises which the dog likes to do in the hope that the cheerful attitude will backwash onto the new action and prevent boredom. The structure of the method you are using is such that it is better not to make the training so appealing at all of the early stages that there will be no opportunities for contention. *To pussyfoot along will cause the dog's resistance to snowball in front until distance and other con-*

28

ditions will make corrections more difficult and unpleasant for the trainer and dog. The demands are reasonable. If they bore your dog, get on his ear and un-bore him. One of the most significant advantages of this method of training is its process of illuminating and dissolving resistance with the short reaches.

You can profitably use several periods each day when working on retrieving if they are separated by at least an hour and you do not change the pattern of objectives until told to do so.

Make only one change as you work on the second day of the one-inch reach. Require the dog to respond to your command eight times without correction before you end each period.

It's about at this level that the dog's improved performance plants a booby trap for the trainer. This trap is baited with overconfidence and is double-jawed. The trainer who fails to have his thumb and the ear in the ready position before giving a command will lose the stability of the pattern and is likely to fumble his way into a correction that demonstrates incompetence instead of authority. One who does not see the value of a lot of practice at each level after the dog has been taken past contention is prone to increase the distance too soon. He's putting a weak block in a foundation that will crumble when strength is needed the most.

Work for several periods each day for the next four days as you did on the second day. At the end of that time, test your dog. Set up two distractions as shown on page 30. Your dog should make five consecutive one-inch reaches between the objects while your thumb is in the ready position, but not exerting pressure.

Start the next level only when your dog has passed the test.

Level 3—Objective: six-inch reach

"Why should I have my dog reach six inches and no farther? Why not progress just as fast as I can?"

Questions such as the above occur to trainers who have not had experience in dividing the exercise into definite blocks, each of which is taught, enforced, practiced and proven before

The use of distractions should begin at the early levels of retrieving.

going on to the next. Perhaps you are asking if the objectives and limitations are not unnecessarily arbitrary. Definitely not! The distances and mechanics for each block have been set by results obtained over many years, and have repeatedly been subjected to the challenge of comparison. Accept no less and ask no more than is specified for each block.

Let's take a look at the significance of the six-inch reach from the dog's viewpoint. In contrast to the transition from merely opening his mouth to the dumbbell to the action of moving his head forward an inch—which required almost no change in the mechanics of the dog's response—the six-inch reach requires a more focused and deliberate move. Though in distance it is a matter of a few inches, the mind of the dog is given the task of making a decision.

Start the lesson by having your dog make a few one-inch reaches, which he is almost certain to do without any pressure from your ever-ready thumb. When he's been praised for the last reach, hold the dumbbell about six inches in front of his mouth and give the command to "Fetch". He will probably reach out to put his mouth over the dumbbell as he has been doing, which will give your right hand a chance to cage his jaws for a few moments of praise.

However, the difference between the mechanical pattern of the short response and the more deliberate move needed to reach the longer distance might cause your dog to hesitate. In such a case, your ready thumb and snugged-up collar should react so fast and effectively that he'll see the advantage of opening and moving his mouth forward without delay. Turn the pressure off and the praise on the instant his mouth covers the dumbbell.

The fact that you've worked the dog past contention at previous levels makes it probable that only a few corrections will be needed before he will perform as willingly on the six-inch reach as he did on the shorter distance. Work during the first period until your dog has made ten responses without correction. They need not be in sequence. Then put him away for a while.

Work your dog according to the above assignment several periods each day for six days. By then your dog should be past contention on the six-inch reach, and ready to be tested for the next level.

Set up two strong distractions, which you have not used previously, about four feet apart. Work your dog between them. When he will make five consecutive reaches without contention he will be ready for the next step.

Level 4—Objective: one-foot reach

The one-foot reach, although it adds but six inches to the pattern the dog has been working, will require another distinct change in his response. If the dumbbell is held a foot in front of his mouth when he is sitting facing forward in a normal position, the dog will have to rise from the SIT to make the reach. To the trainer, the added inches bring an even greater significance. The head of an obstinate dog can no longer be jammed forcefully forward to the dumbbell. There is now space for him to duck, twist about, and veer off before his mouth travels that foot. The trainer will have to brace himself so that he'll be able to stop any gyrations, hold his grip on the collar, keep up the thumb pressure, and force the head straight forward. This can be a bit of a job.

Start the period by having the dog make a few six-inch reaches which will give you an opportunity to praise him. Next, hold the dumbbell a foot from his mouth when he's sitting facing directly forward with his head at the normal level. Give the "fetch" command. Don't let the distance tighten you into putting pressure on the ear if it isn't needed, but be ready. Give him an extra amount of praise if he responds properly the first time. If a correction is needed, move his head all the way to the dumbbell, don't bring the dumbbell to him.

To compromise by moving the dumbbell toward the dog is to declare your willingness to retrieve for him. This can be embarrassing at a later date. I recall one trainer who used to romp out ecstatically after the dumbbell as an example for her dog. She quit training, and became an obedience judge.

End the period when your dog has made a total of five one-foot reaches without correction.

Work until you reach this same quota during each of several daily periods for enough days to bring the dog to a point where he makes the five reaches consecutively.

Test him for readiness to begin the next lesson by asking him to make the five consecutive reaches around the sights and sounds of an area he has not visited before.

Level 5—Objective: to hold the dumbbell

Why wasn't the HOLD started along with the "fetch"? Logic will answer that question.

Part of giving your dog the best possible introduction to the dumbbell was the instant praise he received each time it entered his mouth from the introduction through the present level of the one-foot reach. It is an elemental fact that nothing could be gained by praising the dog for accepting the dumbbell if in that same instant one needed to correct him for dropping it. *The almost simultaneous correction would cancel the effect of the praise.* The only logical procedure is to start the HOLD at this level of training and in a way that would prevent such complications.

Place your dog in a SIT-STAY. Face him from about a foot out in front. Without saying a word, gently put the dumbbell in his mouth exactly as you did at the start of the retrieving exercise (pages 17 and 18). Do not praise him for accepting it—certainly a dog that has reached hundreds of times for a dumbbell no longer needs a reward for merely accepting it. Cage his jaws lightly shut with your right hand and command: "Hold." Keep the dumbbell in his mouth a few seconds before you start to praise him so he'll feel rewarded for holding, not accepting. Because of his familiarity with the dumbbell, he probably will make no effort to expel it, but if he does, continue to hold his mouth shut.

When you've had time to thoroughly associate praise with the dumbbell—roughly, ten seconds—tell him to "Give," and

The text explains the reason for the cradled thumb.

casually take the dumbbell from his mouth. Give him a break of a minute or so and then work him again.

Repeat the above formula of work and breaks a total of eight times during two daily training periods that are separated from the retrieving work by at least a few minutes. These short training periods can be scheduled for odd times and places in order to suit your convenience. After three days, your dog will be prepared for the next level of holding.

Study the picture on page 34 before you attempt to correct your dog for dropping the dumbbell. Note how the thumb of the right hand is cradled tightly in the forefinger. It is this surface that meets the dog's lower jaw when he is chucked sharply under the chin for dropping the dumbbell. The form and feel of your hand used in this manner will have an effect that carries none of the offense of a slap or a blow. It is totally different than any other expression your hand could convey.

Place your dog, put the dumbbell in his mouth, and tell him to hold as you've done previously. Now, instead of preventing him from dropping the dumbbell, have your hand ready for action about four inches below his jaw, as shown in the picture. If he holds the dumbbell long enough to receive your word of praise, move your hand up to take it from him as you say, "Give," then, without any praise for releasing the dumbbell, let him have a break of a minute or so before you repeat the exercise.

If he lets the dumbbell fall from his mouth before you can give him that word of praise, don't try to prevent its dropping. Let it fall. Then bring that carefully poised right hand up with a jolt that pops your cradled thumb sharply against his lower jaw. Quickly put the dumbbell back into his mouth, tell him to "Hold," and position your hand for another correction. Again, if he drops the dumbbell before you have a chance to praise, give him another correction, return the dumbbell to his mouth, and repeat the word "Hold." Work until you get your chance to praise him for a good response, and take the dumbbell from him as you were told to above.

The instruction to repeat the word "Hold" does not contradict the policy of giving only one command for each performance of an exercise. The HOLD, unlike exercises that involve only the dog's movement or position, contends with the additional object of the dumbbell; thus the desired physical situation cannot be established nor reestablished by the simple mechanics of correction. At the present stage, you must return the dropped dumbbell to his mouth, and you will gain more than you will lose by another HOLD command as you do so. *Be careful that you don't anticipate and hit his jaw before the dumbbell clears his mouth, even though you know he's about to drop it. You would be actually correcting him for having it in his mouth—perhaps painfully if the dumbbell cuts his tongue.*

After experiencing the consequences of dropping the dumbbell a few times, your dog will freeze his mouth shut for that second or so. Don't be so slow to recognize his understanding that he'll waver before praise shows him he's doing the right thing. Follow each good response with a few minutes break before you work him again.

Work until you get five or six opportunities to praise him for the short HOLD, then end the period. Two such periods on each of three days should bring your dog a foundation of accomplishment which will make possible a gradual lengthening of the HOLDS. Have definite objectives. On the fourth day gradually increase the time until your dog holds for about five seconds. On the fifth day use your two periods to gradually double that time. Be consistent in your handling techniques as you continue to double the holding time on each of the next three days. By then, your dog will be holding the dumbbell for more than a minute at a time. Occasionally give him some practice in holding for a minute near some distractions.

Until now, you have been facing your dog in a way that implied a readiness to correct. You have done his concentrating for him. It is time to change your position a bit so he'll have to do his own concentrating. Have him hold the dumbbell while you step sidewards, backwards and forwards. After you've convinced him that you'll stop your movements to correct him any time he fumbles, you can begin terminating the exercise by making a complete counter-clockwise circle around him before you reach out to take the dumbbell. After a few days of such work, he'll hold reliably as you move about him.

It is now time to start him moving with the dumbbell in his mouth. Let's take a look at two approaches to carrying a dumbbell which should be avoided.

(1) Giving a dog a dumbbell and telling him to heel. In this case, a correction for dropping the dumbbell might come just as he was giving his best response to the heel command.

(2) Calling a dog from a STAY with a recall command to get him to bring the dumbbell is just as impractical. If the dog did the recall properly he would merit praise even though he dropped the dumbbell on the way.

True, the above methods have sometimes been used successfully but there is another method which combines the highest potential for success with the least possibility of confusion.

Casually stand the dog beside you, but do not tell him to stay. Put the dumbbell in his mouth and tell him to hold. Without further word, ease into the leash to move the dog forward a foot, then stop. If he held the dumbbell for the length of the move, take it and give him a lot of praise. If he dropped it, correct him and move forward again.

Although this policy of moving him without a command causes less confusion than other ways of getting him to move, some dogs will try to use motion as an excuse for dropping a dumbbell. You might have to correct him a few times to convince him he should hold the dumbbell and move at the same time. Persist until he makes six of the short moves with the dumbbell during each of your two daily periods of work on the HOLD during the next few days.

After that much experience, you can gradually lengthen the distance he walks beside you holding the dumbbell. Walk him over rough ground and low obstacles, such as one board in a

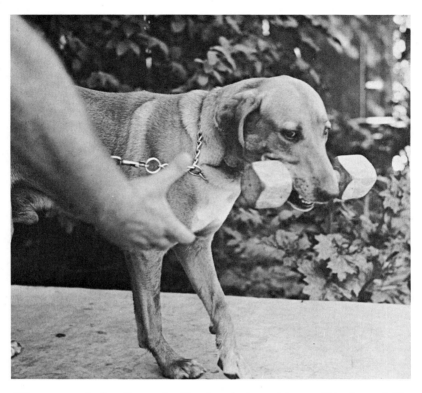

*After an arm's length reach, the dog is brought smoothly toward the
waiting hand.*

regulation high jump, so that he'll get used to the jouncing of the dumbbell.

You must read your dog carefully so that you don't push him too fast nor permit him to be too lax on the carrying exercise. Occasionally, study your own reactions to be sure you are praising and correcting as in the instructions on page 35.

You will soon learn the logical and easy way to combine the HOLD and REACH.

Level 6—Objective: the arm's length retrieve

The act of reaching an arm's length for the dumbbell will give even the biggest dog practice in a pattern of moving his mouth farther than the distance it is to the ground before him. The smaller dogs will also benefit from being asked to reach the same distance.

Start by placing the dog and arranging the collar, ear and thumb just as you did on the shorter reaches. Hold the dumbbell a full arm's length in front of him. Command, "Fetch!"

Be careful not to let a stressing of your left arm as it moves with the long reach cause thumb pressure which should only be applied for a correction.

Your dog will probably reach the increased distance on command and give you a chance to praise him and take the dumbbell. If not, be quick to correct. Do not give him relief until he has moved his open mouth all the way to the dumbbell. Be careful not to move the dumbbell toward him.

During each of the first two daily periods, work until the dog reaches on command for six *consecutive* times. Repeat that assignment each day for a week or until it appears that your dog is infallible in reaching an arm's length on command. Then it will become your responsibility to provide distractions that will make him fail a few times. Nowhere in dog training does the strategy of choosing the battleground pay off better than at this level, which features the final work with the dumbbell before the dog is required to retrieve it from the ground. Each opportunity to correct the dog toward a dumbbell held in the air will lessen the number and difficulty of those periods when he can oppose you with braced legs as you force him toward a dumbbell on the ground. So, in kindness to both of you, work him around a lot of distractions while you still have the mechanical advantage.

In addition to using changes of environment, animals and other objects for distraction, give your dog a new angle of reach. Lower the dumbbell an inch every few REACHES until he's taking it when it is held six inches from the ground. When correcting, don't raise the dumbbell or bring it closer to him. He needs practice in reaching for the dumbbell—not in waiting for it to come to him.

An occasional dog, generally because of tentative or inconsistent handling, will get hung up on this waiting. As soon as the ear pressure starts, he is apt to rocket toward the dumbbell, proving that he knew exactly what was wanted but waited for a physical cue, poor handling having taught him that his dim-witted trainer would probably abort the correction the moment he starts. You can outmaneuver such a waiter.

Give a "Fetch!" command. If he waited for the thumb pressure, oblige him; but hold him back so rigidly that he can't move an inch toward the dumbbell. Keep the pressure up for several seconds regardless of how he spins his drivers or yelps.

Then let him lunge out to get the dumbbell. The moment he takes it, stop the thumb pressure. Such an experience each time he waits will convince him he should respond promptly to the fetch command.

Be careful that your readiness to hold back doesn't cause you to restrict him when he does respond to command.

Do not be concerned if the dog's determination not to be found waiting causes him to jump the gun on your command. *Such anticipation can be corrected later.*

By the time your dog is reaching an arm's length for the dumbbell under the conditions described, you can reasonably begin to combine the FETCH and the HOLD. Instead of stretching out to take the dumbbell from him when he has reached for it, tell him to "Hold," and use your grip on the collar to gently turn him to face you. Then tell him to "Give," and take the dumbbell as soon as he has turned. Probably your previous work on holding and carrying will make such a simple demand seem too easy. Nevertheless, it is a change in the pattern of taking the dumbbell from him, and you can prevent confusion by praising him for his first success in combining the FETCH and HOLD.

If he should drop the dumbbell before you tell him to "Give," correct as instructed on page 37 relative to carrying.

Progressively increase the distance he moves toward you after turning. Within a few days you should be able to bring him all the way in to you, and with a gentle tug and a word cue him to sit. When that step has become a pattern, start conditioning him to wait for a few seconds before you take the dumbbell.

A week of work on the exercises in this lesson should bring your dog to a point where, regardless of environment, he will retrieve the dumbbell from where it is held close to the ground an arm's length from him and hold it until you take it from him after he sits in front of you.

Your dog, regardless of his enthusiasm, will be affected adversely if you start the next lesson before he will perform as described above. Work—don't gamble.

Level 7—Objective: retrieving from the ground

The trainer's policy of honestly evaluating himself and his dog before starting a higher level of training is particularly significant to this lesson. This list of questions will help you in your "inventory."

> (1) Are you consistent in being ready with your collar and thumb positions even though your dog seems almost past the need for correction?
>
> (2) Have you used distractions to prove your dog past contention at each level before starting the next lesson?

Work a lot on three foot retrieves before you lengthen the distance.

(3) Did you give the dog the feeling of progressive successes by holding to the book's order of treating each step as an objective, not just as a temporary foothold in an unfocused struggle toward some remote goal?

When you can answer yes to each of the above questions you are prepared to start this lesson.

Have your dog retrieve the dumbbell a couple of times from an arm's length away and a few inches from the ground. Next, place the dumbbell on the ground at the same distance, and keep your hand on it as shown in the picture. Give the fetch command. Experience should prompt your dog to retrieve as usual. Take the dumbbell and praise him as he lifts it to assure that his first experiment in retrieving from the ground will be a success.

Do not lift the dumbbell from the ground for him.

Give him a break of a minute or so. Repeat the retrieve from the ground in exactly the same way. Five or six of these experiences of retrieving the dumbbell from the ground with your hand on it to tell him that nothing has changed are sufficient for each of the first four training periods.

After the foregoing success, continue to place the dumbbell on the ground the same distance before him, but take your hand from it before you command him to retrieve. Until told otherwise, continue to take the dumbbell as soon as it clears the ground. During each of a half-dozen periods work him as instructed on retrieving the dumbbell without the cue of your hand touching it.

Occasionally there is a dog, up to par on all previous lessons, who chooses to make a last-ditch stand before the monumental concession of retrieving from the ground. Anyone who has trained a number of dogs in practical retrieving, or has watched the process extensively, has seen this resistance take the form of a phenomenon. For example, a dog will start toward a dumbbell on the ground, then pretend he doesn't see it. A correction inspires him to histrionics which sees him cover the dumbbell with his chest and grab a match or a bit of stick on the ground. Is he confused? No. Then why should he do such a thing? Hundreds of identical performances should prove to the most skeptical that a dog often regards retrieving from the ground, when it does not please him to retrieve, as a most significant concession to a trainer's will. The throes and vocal effects are sometimes awe inspiring.

If your dog is one who makes such a last stand, you must win the battle. No matter how violently or how long he thrashes about as he tries to retrieve matches, sticks or your feet, or tries to chew on your hands, stay with your correction. If necessary, use the right hand on the collar and ear, and reach across with your left to grasp the hide on the far side in order to wrestle his mouth to the dumbbell. Don't waver or change your tactics if your dog continues to struggle for a half-hour or more. With his background, he knows what he should do. To settle for less than your reasonable demand now, or to try to bridge across the rough spot with a compromise would result in an infirm motivation that will crumble when it's needed the most.

So that your efforts will not be weakened by the dog's acting nor by prophecies that "you'll break his spirit," or "make him hate the dumbbell," I invite any and all advisors to challenge the substance, details and significance of the affidavit on pages 46 and 47.

The moment your maneuvering and thumb pressure has caused the dog to lift the dumbbell clear of the ground, take it. Your praise should end the session. Possibly you'll both need a rest.

Seldom does a last-stand fighter need more than two or three bouts to favorably change his attitude toward lifting the dumbbell from the ground. Work him enough periods, as instructed above, to gain your objective. If your dog does seem to resist abnormally, be sure your timing of the thumb pressure and praise isn't garbled, or that something else in your handling isn't confusing him.

Above all, be honest in your answer to this question: Did you take the dog past contention and test him at each level of work before going on to the next? If the answer is no, go back and rebuild.

A few periods of good handling based on the right foundation will bring even an obstinate dog to the point of lifting the dumbbell from the ground, much to the amazement of a trainer who has felt that such a time would never come.

As soon as your dog is lifting the dumbbell reliably, start telling him to hold as it clears the ground, and turn him back toward your waiting hand exactly as you did on the arm's length reach.

Observations in my open classes indicate that two training periods each day for a week should take the dog from the first lift to the point where he turns with it to the trainer's hand and gives on command. Practice an extra few days if necessary so the dog will do the exercise without contention before you start the next level.

Level 8—Objective: the leash-length retrieve

Start by having the dog make a few retrieves just as he did at the close of the last lesson. After you've had the chance to praise him a few times, increase the distance by one foot from the dog to where you place the dumbbell. It is now, before the dog is sent the increased distance, that an important change in handling technique should be described.

Have the thumb in the ready position as you prepare for the command. *Now concentrate so that your handling will be smooth.* If the dog starts on command, release the ear and collar and let him make the retrieve. Your leash must be loose until he has picked up the dumbbell, but then tighten gently to encourage him to retrieve to your waiting hand. Promptly tell him, "Joe, give," and take the dumbbell from him so that you won't miss an opportunity to praise him for retrieving the increased distance. If the dog balks at the increase, apply the pressure and don't release it until he lifts the dumbbell.

You might encounter the problem of having your dog respond to your command and then, when you've removed your hand

AFFIDAVIT

To Whom It May Concern:

I, Margaret Pooley, residing at 2104 S. Cucamonga Ave., Ontario, California, do hereby warrant and represent as follows:

That I have observed, as a participant and a bystander, the retrieving methods of W. R. Koehler employed in dog training classes for more than twenty years, during which period I saw hundreds of dogs of many different breeds trained to retrieve;

That a method of positive motivation was used to cause the dogs to retrieve under increasingly distracting and unfavorable conditions, which included various kinds of scents, animals and close proximity to city traffic;

That I cannot recall any dog who participated in a full course, of no more than twelve weeks duration, that was not brought to the point of retrieving reliably;

That it was obvious that dogs who had no background in ball playing or natural retrieving, including those who were by nature the most violently opposed to the exercise, were at the conclusion of the course generally among the happiest retrievers.

That many participants, including myself, have used this positively motivated retrieving to bring increased confidence and other character benefits to dogs.

46

As evidence of my qualifications to make the above statements on the teaching and use of a retrieving method, I submit the statistics on dogs that I have qualified for Obedience titles:

I have qualified:
23 dogs for the title of Companion Dog
16 dogs for the title of Companion Dog Excellent
 5 dogs for the title of Utility Dog

Thirteen of the above numbers were also awarded the title of Champion by reason of qualification in the conformation classes.

The above statistics are substantiated by the records of the American Kennel Club.

Margaret Pooley

TO 447 C
(Individual)

STATE OF CALIFORNIA
COUNTY OF _San Bernardino_ } SS.

On _10-17-69_ before me, the undersigned, a Notary Public in and for said State, personally appeared _Margaret Pooley_ _____

_____, known to me

to be the person _S_ whose name _is_ subscribed to the within instrument and acknowledged that _she_ executed the same.

WITNESS my hand and official seal.

Signature_____

_____
Name (Typed or Printed)

OFFICIAL SEAL
ANTHONY G. PEICH
NOTARY PUBLIC - CALIFORNIA
PRINCIPAL OFFICE IN
SAN BERNARDINO COUNTY
My Commission Expires March 21, 1973

(This area for official notarial seal)

from the ready position, decide against making the retrieve until your hand returns to his collar. *Do not let him outsmart you by retrieving just as you recover the means of correcting him.* Instead, hold him back so that his evasion doesn't start a pattern. Then make a correction. Do not weaken his sense of responsibility by giving a second command. Let your correction strengthen his concentration.

When your dog retrieves without contention over the new distance you can add another foot to the pattern. Proceed with the exercise just as before. Be sure to keep slack in the leash except when correcting, so your dog won't be jerked to a stop just as he is trying to please you. *Until told otherwise, do not command your dog to retrieve when he is off the leash.*

Give your dog enough practice to take him past contention at each distance as you progressively increase the length of the retrieve to four or five feet. You should reach the objective within a week, but be certain that your dog qualifies before you go on to the next level.

Level 9—Objective: increasing reliability

Start the first step by giving the dog a bit of practice in retrieving the distance reached in the last lesson. When you've praised him for making a half-dozen consecutive retrieves take him, still on leash, into a situation that he might find moderately distracting: near an open car door, a strange person, etc. Place him on a SIT-STAY beside you. Toss your dumbbell a slack leash-length away and within a few feet of the distraction. Give the command, and if your dog moves to retrieve in the face of the distraction let go of his collar and make sure the leash doesn't tighten as he goes toward the dumbbell. If necessary, use the leash to gently bring him to a sitting position in front of you. Take the dumbbell and praise his good performance.

Be quick to correct if your dog is distracted by a situation such as the one pictured.

Remember: if because of the distraction, or for any other reason, your dog stops short of getting the dumbbell, hold him where he stopped so that he can't make a frantic scramble to retrieve just ahead of your correction. Calmly and deliberately work your way down the leash, arrange the collar and ear and apply a pressure that doesn't stop until he lifts the dumbbell. Then finish the exercise in the normal manner.

The praise he has received for fetching and carrying, along with the corrections you gave for dropping the dumbbell, have made your dog understand he should hold the dumbbell until he is told to give. From now on, if he drops the dumbbell you will no longer correct him as you've done in the past. Instead, snub him up with the leash while you arrange the collar and thumb, and then correct him all the way to the dumbbell as though he hadn't started on command. Do not repeat the command—he knows what he should do. He should be made to pick up the dumbbell each time he drops it, even if it means a dozen corrections on a single retrieve.

Work your dog near the same distraction until he performs without contention, generally a matter of five or six retrieves. Then do the same in another distracting situation. Three separate situations, which would add up to fifteen or twenty retrieves, should be enough for the first period. Two such periods each day for ten days should have the dog retrieving on leash without contention under conditions that are more distracting than a dog would normally encounter.

So far, because of the need to let your dog savor to the fullest the praise he has earned by retrieving, he has been permitted to enjoy his reward without interruption after responding to your command to give. By now it is logical to give him a word of praise for retrieving, and complete the exercise by having him finish to your left side as you did on the novice recall.

Practice the exercise for as many daily periods as are necessary before you leave the convenience of the six-foot training leash.

Level 10—Objective: the formal pattern

By now your dog has had sufficient experience in retrieving so that he will not be confused as you make three essential changes in your handling. They are:
  (1) Correcting the dog for anticipation
  (2) Sending your dog without the thumb being in the ready position
  (3) Handling in the formal manner as is required in the obedience trials

The American Kennel Club's rules on how a handler and dog must perform on the retrieving exercises are often resented by those who fail to see that the exacting demands have a value other than merely establishing the uniform patterns necessary for judging. The requirement that the dog respond immediately to the "Fetch!" command and, without additional cue, retrieve to a sitting position in front of the handler and hold the dumbbell until the judge permits the handler to take it, rounds out quite a test of the dog's responsibility.

Begin the period by putting the dumbbell inside your shirt so your hands will be free to handle the leash and correct for inaccuracy. Bring your dog at heel to the place where you will start the exercise. If the dog fails to sit automatically with speed and accuracy, correct for the disobedience just as you do on any stop with the dog at heel. Remember—in the OPEN RING there will not even be the presence of a leash to influence your dog, nor can you use the collar to adjust the dog's position, so demand good performance while you still have the opportunity to correct.

Once the dog sits accurately, hold the leash in your left hand, allowing two feet of slack, and hold that hand rigidly against your leg. Give a STAY command. Take the dumbbell from your shirt and without looking at the dog toss it a leash length in front of him. Immediately bring your throwing hand back to hang at your side. If the dog takes the motion of your arm and the dumbbell as a signal to fetch, let him be jerked to a stop by the two feet of leash, then use both hands to correct him back to the SIT-STAY without any repetition of command.

Again, stand in position with hands at your sides and the two feet of slack in the leash. This time, with the dumbbell already lying on the ground, there'll be no motion, and the dog will probably hold. If not, correct again. When he has held for a few seconds, give the command to fetch, remaining motionless except to provide the full length of leash when he responds to your command. To fail to give him the full slack when he takes your command would be a cruelty.

If your formal attitude and the absence of your hand from his collar causes him to delay his response to your command, or if he starts for the dumbbell but doesn't follow through, hold him back with the leash while you arrange the collar and ear, then correct him all the way to the dumbbell. As said before, don't let him outmaneuver you with a quick lunge toward the dumbbell when he sees you move. Your move shouldn't serve as a second command: it's the start of a correction that will result inevitably from each failure to respond.

The next parts of the retrieving exercise, which are best polished in unison, are the dog's prompt pickup and firm handling of the dumbbell. Insist that the dog pick up the dumbbell as soon as he gets to it, while you can jump in and make quick corrections, because any fault of dawdling will be worsened by distance. If he plays with the dumbbell or holds it insecurely, pull him in so rapidly with the leash that he won't have time to mouth it.

Don't excuse a fumble caused by the force of the pull or a bump from the leash. Get on the collar and ear and correct as you would for any drop. Make an issue of it while he's working close and you have the opportunity to do so. The slow pickup and the dawdling, fumbling return can be corrected within a couple of days.

Regardless of the reason for pulling him toward you, see that the dog ends up sitting straight in front of you so the dumbbell can be reached without strain. In addition to align-

52

ing him with a leash correction, you can dress him up sharply with hand chops to his sides as is commonly done when teaching the novice RECALL. He should sit before you without mouthing or dropping the dumbbell until you tell him "Give," when he should let you take it without any reluctance or horseplay. A mouth-opening pinch on the lips should be sufficient to correct for a slow release. The mouth of an obstinate dog will nearly always eject a dumbbell or bird when the handler blows hard in his ear. If he tries to back off with the dumbbell to play games, give him a stiff leash correction back to where he should be sitting. After you take the dumbbell, he should continue to hold the SIT until your command, "Joe, heel," orders him to do the finish.

Each day as you use the above mechanics on the leash-length retrieves, wait a few seconds longer between the toss of the dumbbell and your command to fetch, and between the time the dog sits in front of you and you take the dumbbell.

A week of handling in the formal pattern should take your dog past contention on all parts of the exercise and prepare you both for working at distances where correction can be difficult.

Before you go to the next level of retrieving, carefully consider this fact: for a dog to start before a command, or to fail to respond to a single command, will mean that he will fail the exercise. By practicing acceptable handling procedures from this point on, whenever the essence of the training moment will permit, you will avoid forming poor handling habits that will be hard to eliminate later. One such fault, very common, is leaning or otherwise gesturing toward the dumbbell when a dog fails to respond to the FETCH, instead of showing him that hesitancy will bring inescapable correction. Another common fault is that of a handler grabbing a dumbbell before a fumbling dog drops it, rather than letting the dog experience the consequences of his irresponsibility.

There are reasons aplenty for you to concentrate on becoming a good handler as well as a good trainer.

Level 11—Objective: transition to off-leash retrieving

Your dog will come to retrieve with great reliability under all kinds of conditions if you concentrate on getting the most from each of the steps that lead from on-leash to off-leash retrieving.

The first step in the transition from on-leash to off-leash retrieving is methodical practice with the dog on the twenty-foot longe line. Handle and correct your dog as you did when he was on leash, even when greater distances make the task more complicated.

Begin by practicing five-foot retrieves until your dog has performed willingly about a half-dozen consecutive times. Next, toss your dumbbell about three feet farther. Be sure that the dog has enough slack, and send him. The chances are he'll perform as usual. Don't be so intent on a prompt and accurate finish that you adulterate the praise he earned by that lengthened retrieve.

A good trainer never loses the opportunity to praise for the essence of the moment rather than to correct for something of lesser importance.

If your dog should take the added distance as an excuse not to respond, or stops short of the dumbbell, you must convince him that distance does not lessen his responsibility. Above all, don't be one of those handlers whose dog gets confused by the drag of the longe line. "Un-confuse" him. Condition him to take difficulty in stride. Because of the foundation you've built, he'll probably go from one or two corrections to retrieving without contention over the new distance. Work him five or six periods at practicing success, then work him for one period over the same distance around a few distractions.

When you feel your dog is solid on the above length, add another three feet to the length of the retrieve, and repeat the same format of success and the challenge of distractions. A week of progressing by this method should have your dog retrieving willingly a slack longe length. Continue to work sys-

54

Use lots of distractions on the longe line work.

The tab and light line.

tematically at this level until you believe that no reasonable situation would alter your dog's reliable performance. Only then will you and your dog be ready for the final step in the transition to off-leash control.

It is at this level of training in properly conducted classes in open work and field work that exclamations are heard. They generally start with the remarks of the trainer of what had promised to be the class blockhead, who had scoffed at the proposition that his reluctant dog would probably become one of the happiest retrievers instead of suffering the inhibitions which had been prophesied by the *commiserados*.

"But why did he fight it so?" is the question asked by all who watched resistance replaced by enthusiasm.

Anyone who has seen how a light line and tab can foil the plans of the most dedicated bolter can easily understand how the same device can convince a dog that it is much better to retrieve when told than to try to outrun the thumb. If it's your first experience with the line and tab, you will soon realize that even the finest mathematician could not figure his chances of avoiding correction when they are used.

The "tab" can be made of a short length of material cut from your longe line. When doubled and looped to the ring as shown on page 56 it should be long enough to grip with one hand, but no longer.

A light line made of one of the new materials need be no larger than $1/8$ inch in diameter to stop the biggest dog, and suitably less for smaller dogs. How long? You will get the answer from a close study of how the equipment is used, but one hundred feet is a good starting length.

To stop those "Yah, but. . . ." handlers who get their kicks from leaving the path of continuity to chase some weird hypothesis I'll contrive an example of a dog that would pose the maximum in difficulty. Assume that the dog is tougher than a terrier, and can run faster than a greyhound, and is hard to convince. You are going to work him.

Attach the line and tab as shown in the picture. The mechanics of handling on the exercise will be exactly the same as they were at the completion of the previous step, except for precautions against the light line cutting you. Don't try to hold it in your hand. It should lie behind you in loose skeins.

Start by having the dog retrieve a few times over a distance of four or five feet, then add a yard each time until he's going as far as when on the longe line. The dog was solid by the end of the last lesson so he should work willingly. But if a correction is needed, step on the line, then work your way down it until you can grab the tab so the correction won't hurt you more than it does the dog. End the period when the dog is performing smoothly at the farthest distance mentioned.

The next period should duplicate the first.

Start the third period with a few of the short retrieves, then toss the dumbbell a bit further on each exercise until the dog is required to fetch it from a distance of about fifty feet. It is now that distance and the lightness of the line will probably combine to give him that out-of-reach feeling which might encourage him to neglect his job. Because we're using an example that will squelch the "Yah, buts," let's suppose that when the dog gets the dumbbell he decides to dodge through your hedge, run through the neighbor's fish pond and onto his porch. In such a case, jump on the line, get your grip, wearing gloves if necessary, and hand-over-hand drag him off the porch, back through the fish pond and the hedge until you can lock onto the tab. If the line is wrapped around an obstacle, work your way to where you can grab the tab. In either case, no matter how long it takes or how much the dog resists, calmly and methodically get your collar and thumb into position and correct him all the way to the dumbbell.

Do not take the dumbbell from him when he lifts it. Instead, without leading him along with you, walk back to where the exercise started, then reel him in to a sitting position in front of you and finish the exercise in the usual way.

Repeat the pattern of the exercise exactly. This time your dog will probably earn your praise for a good retrieve. If not, correct as before. Work until he willingly makes a few of the long retrieves, then end the period. During the next four or five periods, progressively lengthen the distance he retrieves to a hundred feet.

Experience might show that you can get along with less than the hundred feet of light line, or that you might require more.

One fact is obvious: there are saltwater fishing lines light enough, strong enough, and long enough to foil the fastest problem dog, although one can hardly conceive of a handler so slow of mind and movement as to need one.

The fact that a dog can't avoid a correction is only one of the advantages of using the light line. The necessity to obey, and the praise obedience brings, will soon have your dog past contention on his retrieves. Then it will be time to subject him to the challenge of unusual situations and distractions as you did at previous levels.

Work for enough periods to take the dog to a point where it seems neither distance nor distractions affect his retrieving on the line. His reliability brings us to the second advantage of the light line: the dog isn't aware of how long it is. He knows that it has always been long enough. Now you can start the procedure of gradually shortening it. For your own feeling of security, work for one period with half the length. You will notice that the dog is unaware of the change in weight. As your confidence in his reliability grows, cut the line back a few feet at a time to a length of five feet. The tab will do such a good job of obscuring the slight changes in the feel of the line that your dog won't be aware of its decreasing length.

If during the line work you have one of those rare experiences where the line snags on something sharp just as you're moving in for a correction and then parts in the way that tells the dog he's free to run, you will have to do a lot of hard and careful work to convince him that he shouldn't try to break the line each time he gets into that same kind of situation.

Repeatedly set up the conditions just as they were when the accident occurred, excepting for changes that would protect against another break in the line, and work until he's convinced that even his wildest attempts will never succeed in breaking the line again. Tempt him to make so many unsuccessful runs that distractions seem only to turn his mind to the responsibility of retrieving. This is a lot of work but it is the only way to cancel out his memory of that one successful run.

When your dog is past contention under all kinds of conditions while dragging only a few feet of line, it will occur to you that he is actually working without physical restraint. For example, if he is sent fifty feet for a dumbbell, he could run as easily while dragging a few feet of line as he could without it. But even though your dog is past the point where he might try to run from a responsibility, let the tab be attached for a while longer as a convenient handle when he might need a correction.

Remember: the assurance of a dog's good performance comes from working under abnormally distracting conditions, when you have the means of physical enforcement, until the dog is completely past contention, so that he will not need a correction when he is free of physical control.

When you feel that he is absolutely reliable, you can start to work him without the tab.

If at this time, or years later, some freakish situation should cause your dog to run from impending correction, you can remedy the problem with the light line. Equip your dog with a line long enough and strong enough to stop any rush. Then do your very best to con him into disobeying as you make the problem situation stronger than it ever was. Make your correction a memorable one. When he sees the hopelessness of trying to outrun you, give him a few extra periods in which to enjoy praise for his success. Then in a fair and reasonable manner increase the distractions in an effort to get him to goof again. Only when you are convinced that no amount of pressure could invite your dog to outrun correction is it advisable to start the pattern of reducing the line length. To remove the entire line in one operation, instead of gradually reducing it would be a senseless gamble.

Congratulations! Inch by inch, you've brought your dog to where he retrieves reliably. It might well be that those observers who wailed, above the dog's occasional yelp, that you would "break his spirit" are a bit disappointed by the enthusiasm, as well as the reliability, with which your dog retrieves.

It's your turn now. Suggest that the advisors work their dogs in comparison with yours—down near the railroad when a freight is rumbling by. Then ask them to explain their theories again.

In appropriate sections of this book are instructions for improving and using the retrieving exercise. They will enable you to get the most benefit from the sound foundation you have built.

Open Training for a hunting dog pays off, both in and out of the field.

2

The Retrieving Exercises

The Retrieve on the Flat

YOUR dog will be well prepared to do the RETRIEVE ON
THE FLAT when you have completed the assignments given
in the material on basic retrieving. Suggestions for polishing
your handling and the dog's performance so as to get the highest possible scores are presented in Chapter 7.

The Retrieve Over the High Jump

Your dog should not be sent to retrieve over a single board
until he has had six weeks of foundation work in correctly
negotiating the jumps. Logically, you should start the separate
process of accustoming him to the jumping pattern at about
the same time you begin work on retrieving, so that by the
time the dog is retrieving a leash length on the flat, you can
reasonably ask him to retrieve over one board in the obstacle.

Set up your hurdle with only the bottom board, which will
stand eight inches above the ground. If you do not yet have
access to a set of jumps, use a board or another substitute of
about the same height, using improvised standards to give it an
authentic appearance. Next, walk in a circle with the dog at

heel in a path that takes you over the jump each time around. Don't say anything the first few times you go over the obstacle in your path. But when the dog shows his understanding of the pattern, speed up to a trot and say, "Over," each time he starts his jump in order to associate the word with the action and condition him to clear the board without touching. He'll enjoy this jumping, so take him over the board with the "Over" about two dozen times each day for a week.

The first week's work on jumping the hurdle will give your dog enough pleasant experience to prevent him from being discouraged by a simple addition you'll make, which will be a wire stretched across between the standards about two inches above the board.

Warning: to prevent an injury from the dog's foot getting caught, rig the wire with a belly of slack as shown in the picture page 65. This wire will help to convince the dog that a clean jump is the best way across the board.

Start the work of the second week by going around the familiar pattern a few times. Then face the jump from a few steps away with the dog sitting at heel. Give the command, "Joe, over," and start on the left foot at a run over the jump to cause an instant response to your command. Repeat these fast patterns so that your speed, together with the wire, will condition your dog to clear the board with a good margin. If your dog is of such a size that his normal movement would keep him unaware of the wire at such a low level, add one board—no more—and place the wire above it. Two dozen of these patterns each day for a week should prepare the dog for the next step.

The fact that you've jumped with the dog in association with the command for two weeks makes it certain that he'll know what "Over!" means. It's time to teach him to respond without the cue of your movement. Put him in close focus to the jump by standing only one step back from the board. Have about a foot of slack in the leash. Without any motion, give the command, "Joe, over!"

If the dog jumps on command, follow through after him so

The slack wire discourages touching the board.

Lots of "Over and back."

fast that he'll know he made exactly the right decision, and butter him up with a lot of praise.

If because of confusion or slowness he doesn't respond instantly, lunge over the jump in a way that uses up the one foot of slack so fast that the dog will wish he had not waited. About ten of these opportunities to learn the advantages of prompt response each day for a week should bring your dog to the point where he jumps before the leash can tighten.

Until you are instructed otherwise, never ask your dog to jump the hurdle—even in play—unless he is on the leash.

In order to get a qualifying score on the RETRIEVE OVER HIGH JUMP the dog must take the jump both going to the dumbbell and returning with it, which makes it advisable to give your dog practice in lining up with the jump when returning to you.

Start by standing with the dog beside you a step back from the jump just as you did at the last level. Command the dog to jump. As you follow through to confirm his judgment, be prepared to make some changes. Pause when your leading foot hits the ground on the far side of the board, but handle the leash in a way that won't jerk the dog when you stop. Give him a word of praise for his jump. Now say, "Back," and as you do step back smoothly across the jump to where you can sit him in front of you. Praise him for his cooperation, then have him FINISH. Now trot over the jump with him and circle back to where you can repeat the exercise. Such a run over the jump between the over and back exercises can help keep the short patterns from making him work in a slow and inhibited manner.

As you work to familiarize your dog with the mechanics of jumping the hurdle, do not worry that the commands of "Over," and "Back," will cause confusion later in the ring where you will not be able to use the words, or that the pattern of starting back to you the moment he lands will cause the dog to turn short of the dumbbell. Long before he's ready

"Tiger" waited too long.

for the ring, the retrieving motivation will be so strong that one or two corrections will place all parts of the exercises in orderly perspective for him.

Regardless of how perfectly the dog responds to your "Over" command, continue that one step across the board so that the dog can go a leash length before he is turned, and say, "Back," as you step backward to strengthen his response to the word. Later, when you start the dog retrieving over the hurdle, you will find "Back" will be one of the most important words in your training vocabulary.

Your success in familiarizing your dog with the jumps has probably been paralleled by your dog's progress in retrieving. When he is doing the jump exercise in a relaxed manner, and is retrieving reliably amid distractions at a leash-length distance, you are prepared to combine the two functions in the RETRIEVE OVER THE HIGH JUMP exercise. Setting up your dog's first experience in retrieving over an obstacle is very critical. Follow instructions carefully.

Stand, with the dog sitting at heel, one step back from the hurdle which should not be more than a single board high. Tell the dog to stay. Hold the leash in your left hand while you step up close to the board and drop the dumbbell about one-and-a-half the dog's length on the other side of the board. Give the dog the "Fetch!" command, making no motion as you do so.

The chances are very good that your dog will retrieve the dumbbell, and his closeness to the hurdle on both sides of the board will influence him to jump both ways. Don't adulterate the praise for this first retrieve by making any corrections for a poor SIT in front of you. Take the dumbbell from him, praise him, and have him FINISH.

If he doesn't respond to your "Fetch" command, or fails to retrieve to you, correct for errors in the usual way.

In case he picks up the dumbbell and stands looking at you, or starts around the hurdle, command, "Back," and tighten the leash to bring him to you or to foul him on the standard, whichever the situation demands. It's his own fault if fouling his head on the standard causes him to drop the dumbbell, so correct as for any other drop.

Consider the value of the word *back*. You must understand that to call a confused dog to you with the word *come* when he is supposed to retrieve would require only that he do a RECALL. Obviously, you could not fairly correct him for dropping the dumbbell. Nor would repeating the word *fetch* indicate to him that he should retrieve over the board. You told him to fetch when you sent him. Use the word *back* to tell him to return across the board.

Not, "Come," not a repeated, "Fetch." Say, "Back." B-A-C-K—*back*.

When your dog is retrieving reliably over the obstacle in a short pattern, replace the leash with your longe line so that you can progressively increase the distance that you stand back from the hurdle while you toss the dumbbell a short distance across the board.

In progressing toward where you'll stand, and where you'll toss the dumbbell, bear in mind that for most breeds the regulations specify:

> "The High Jump shall be jumped clear, and the jump shall be as nearly as possible one and one-half times the height of the dog at the withers, with a minimum height of 8 inches, and a maximum height of 36 inches."

Exceptions, as noted, have been allowed for the following breeds: Bloodhounds, Bullmastiffs, Great Danes, Great Pyrenees, Mastiffs, Newfoundlands, and St. Bernards need jump only *once* the height of the dog at the withers or 36 inches, whichever is less. Clumber Spaniels, Sussex Spaniels, Basset Hounds, Dachshunds, Pembroke and Cardigan Welsh Corgis, Australian Terriers, Cairn Terriers, Dandie Dinmont Terriers, Norwich Terriers, Scottish Terriers, Sealyham Terriers, Skye Terriers, West Highland White Terriers, Maltese, Pekingese, Bulldogs, and French Bulldogs need jump just once the height of the dog at the withers, or 8 inches, whichever is greater.

Regulations give the handler ". . . the option of standing any reasonable distance from the High Jump, but must stay

Setting up the first retrieve over the High Jump.

in the same spot throughout the exercise." This means that the distance most favorable for you will be determined by the size of your dog, and his style of jumping.

A book covering all of the Regulations for Obedience Trials, which also includes descriptions of acceptable ring equipment and much other useful information, can be obtained free of charge from the American Kennel Club, 51 Madison Avenue, New York, N. Y. 10010. (See Appendix for excerpts.)

Common sense, practise, and close observation will enable you to determine the best pattern of working your dog.

There are two schools of thought on the tossing technique. One advocates gripping the dumbbell by one of its bells and tossing it with a bit of backspin so that it will land without a roll. The other advises balancing the shaft across the palm and tossing it so it lands flat, lateral to its line of flight, and does not bounce on an end. Try both ways—and on all kinds of surfaces.

In daily periods, separate from working with the dumbbell, give your dog extra experience in the over and back work on the hurdle. Add a board, and others if they are needed to progress toward the height that your dog will be required to jump in the ring.

Remember: Failure to bring your dog to a point of maximum reliability in jumping heights that you can easily step over when correcting is to share the sad lot of those handlers who struggle to correct their inadequacies by pitching their dogs back and forth across a hurdle that is too high for a person to step over.

Your dog should be completely past contention on jumping at each level of increase before he is asked to retrieve over that height lest you trap yourself into having to correct on both the retrieve and jump at the same time.

While you are still working on the longe line at the convenient lower levels, include a lot of practice around distractions.

Don't forget to condition your dog against the distractions of scent which will occur in the ring. You can accomplish this

72

Run beside the jump as you accustom the dog to more boards.

Give the dog lots of practise in realigning with the jump.

by subjecting your dog to scents that are more appealing than any the dog would encounter in the ring environment, and correcting him for any lapse in responsibility. Bear, raccoon, fox, coyote and wildcat scents are all good temptations. After a few effective corrections, the more exotic the smell your dog encounters the more it will turn his mind back to his job. All of these scents and many more can be obtained for convenient use from the National Scent Company, at the address given on page 141.

Include much practice in having the dog retrieve a dumbbell that has been tossed to a spot out of line with the jump so that he must concentrate on realigning himself for the return trip. A few bad experiences in fouling the line on a standard will make him work with deliberation instead of by rote.

Continue to work, separately from the retrieving exercises, to gradually increase the height of the jump until he does the "over and back," on leash or longe, with the boards set about two inches higher than he will be required to jump in the ring. Only when he is familiar with jumping each gradual increase in height will it be reasonable to ask him to retrieve over the same level.

When your dog retrieves reliably over the required height under difficult conditions, and corrections are so seldom needed that you no longer require the grip afforded by the longe, continue to practice with the light line and tab you used when working on the RETRIEVE ON THE FLAT. It is so light as to give the feeling of freedom but is long enough and strong enough to prevent him from out-running the seldom-needed corrections. Even after you've convinced him that it's always better to retrieve properly than to fail, you will gain by working him with the tab as a convenient handle until you feel that his concentration rules out any mental lapses.

The author prepares "The Ugly Dachshund" for the chariot race in the Walt Disney film based on the classic story by G. B. Sterne.

3

The Heel Free

IT is to be assumed that anyone about to begin OPEN training has brought his dog so far past contention with NOVICE work that, regardless of the distraction, the dog would not consider breaking and running from the heel position. If you and your dog are not qualified to that extent, retrace your Novice heeling. If your basic work depended solely on repetition, as a substitute for systematically working for off-leash control, I would suggest that you use the method presented in the author's book on NOVICE work: *The Koehler Method of Dog Training.* It is always a great disservice to offer only parts of a training method so, advisedly, you are referred to the complete text instead of being offered partial explanations.

The HEEL FREE EXERCISE in OPEN, except for the inclusion of the figure 8, is fundamentally the same as in the Novice ring, but there are important differences in degree, if not in kind. There is more opportunity for heeling faults to occur in the Open ring and they are more noticeable. By focusing on each fault and its correction one can prepare a dog for higher scoring in the ring and enhance his value as a companion.

The "Geared" Dog

"Geared" is another way of describing the dog who is commonly called high-strung or restless. He is wound so tight that he can hardly relax. He would pant just as hard on an ice flow at sixty below zero as he would on a summer day. On or off leash he is no more companionable than a case of hives. If he's a hunting dog, you may be sure he'll be more of a liability than an asset in the field. In the obedience ring, he is particularly unpleasant to handle on the HEEL FREE EXERCISE as he foams along a foot or so out in front of the handler. He loses points through body contact on the left turns, and has to waddle backwards into position on the automatic SITS. Certainly the seriousness of the fault warrants all of a handler's efforts to correct it, and justifies the considerable space this book allots to help in those efforts.

Start by reviewing the novice leash work, particularly those hard left turns into the dog. If it begins to appear that your bruised and battered knee will give way before the left turns could influence your dog, you will have to go a different route. This correction is in the nature of a formula that uses a distraction that will have great appeal to your dog, a lot of time and an open mind—yours. Be sure when you make the set-up that no other distractions than the one you've chosen are present. Just as a concentrated focus is better in hypnotism and brainwashing, it is better in our formula.

With your dog at heel, approach the set-up at a bit slower than normal pace and by such a path that his first sight of the distraction comes as a surprise to him. The moment he alerts, sneak to a stop and let his torque and the temptation pull him still farther out in front of you. Before he can make one of his delayed SITS, or back into position, explode in a SIT correction, using legs, body and arms, that jerks him airborne to the correct SIT position beside you. Distance permitting, give a heel command and move closer to the distraction. Again, when he eases ahead, sneak to a stop and correct before he has a chance to adjust of his own volition.

Remember—the purpose of the formula is not to reward his readjustment by omitting a correction but, rather, to discourage each breach of position. How fascinating to watch a dimwitted handler pardon a dog that's clever enough to readjust ahead of a correction. Such a dog gets steadily better at readjusting and steadily worse at holding the proper position.

If space allows, make another start toward the distraction and repeat the stop and correction. Probably, as you draw close, the temptation will have become an object of suspicion to the dog and he'll begin to hang back. At such a time make a right-about turn and stop abruptly. If the dog overshoots the heel position as he sweeps around you, make a correction that tells him he had better be prepared to sit in the proper position whenever you stop after a change of direction. To do less would be to nourish his torque by allowing him to express himself with a wild rush or jump from inattentiveness to recovery each time you turn right or about. A "geared" dog will generally make a game of foiling attempts to surprise him with turns by literally scrambling around before a handler's change of direction can tighten the leash with a jolt. His scramble toward the new direction will nearly always carry him past the correct position. It is at such times that a quick stop catches him in the middle of a scramble and "unscrambles" him.

Next, take one step with the dog at heel, do an about turn and another stop with the honest hope that you can get in another correction. Now that you are facing back toward the distraction, you can repeat the above described pattern of approaches and stops. Run the pattern at least ten times the first day. If by the end of the session the dog has begun to regard the situation as one where he will be most comfortable when he concentrates on holding the correct heel position, the patterns would seem to be helping to suppress him. Thus encouraged, work the same number of patterns each day for as many days as it takes for the balm of concentration to relax your dog.

Remember: Just one inconsistent moment of letting the left hand restrain the leash communicatively, instead of responding to his forgetfulness with a proper correction, will cancel out hours of hard work.

Ironically, many owners of "geared" dogs believe that the grinding, panting torque is the result of insufficient exercise and try to relieve the stress with orgies of ball-playing. Generally, their dogs are made higher and higher by the practice. There is a contrary course which of itself provides varying degrees of benefits, and which should also be employed as an adjunct to the other techniques that are used to unwind a "geared" dog. It is the simple practice of having the dog hold extra long SIT-STAYS and DOWN-STAYS under distracting conditions.

An occasional "geared" dog, too insensitive to be affected by his master's use of the conventional corrections, can be calmed by the use of a heeling-post such as shown on page 81. The post can be of metal or wood in any diameter from three inches to a foot. Regardless of your dog's size, it must be at least three feet high. One post can be used to serve the purpose, but three set firmly in the ground about eight feet apart will be more convenient. The formula for effective use is simple but rigid. *Do exactly as instructed.*

With the dog at heel, approach the area on a line with the post or posts. Be sure to have the usual amount of heeling slack in the leash, and by your normal gait and every other means encourage the dog to fudge his usual foot or so out in front. Carefully make an alignment that will influence the heedless dog to pass on the left side of the post as you pass on the right. Obviously, the post will foul the leash at a point between you. Do not slow down, compromise, or in any other way warn the dog of what impends. Just as his neck passes on the far side of the post, lock your hand against your stomach and speed up until you feel him bump against the opposite side of the post, then slow to your normal walk and angle a bit to the right so that it is possible for his head to come grating around from the far side of the post in a way that causes

One experience is generally enough.

discomfort. Try to duplicate the set-up on the next post.

Probably on the second try, when your dog is several feet from the post, you will have one of the most shocking experiences of your life as he hangs back or presses very close to you, flatly refusing to be "drifted" toward the wrong side, and indicating by his position and attentiveness that he wants nothing to come between you.

Because you might be shocked by the meaning of such a happening and be asking whether a dog trainer could be aware of the shattering significance of such incontrovertible evidence of a dog's reasoning power, we'll take time out to tell you that dog trainers have long been aware of the following facts:

(1) In 80% of the instances where a dog brings discomfort on himself by fouling his leash on a post or tree while his uncompromising handler bulls forward, he learns from one experience to avoid future traps.

(2) The actual learning time in which a dog's head contacts the post and comes grating around to the right side averages about one second.

(3) Controlled experiments have proven that no combination of patient teaching reward and carefully applied correction will produce a result equal to a moment's encounter with the inviolable laws of physics.

(4) The fact that almost any dog once caught on the wrong side of the post will avoid a second experience by a deliberate scramble that prevents the leash from fouling, thus proving that a dog's reasoning power will override an instinct that would have him flinch back from the point of danger, in the manner of a hand avoiding a hot object.

(5) The 20% of the dogs who, because of a lesser capacity or mis-timing in handling, do not learn from their first contact with the post will learn from a few more experiences.

82

(6) The process and result described above disprove the psychology laboratory concept of several areas of a dog's mentality by showing that a dog, when properly motivated, will learn from one experience to solve a complex problem in mechanics.

The therapy that the heeling post will bring to your "geared" dog will come not from the speed of his learning, but rather from the calming effect of much practice in attentiveness. Give him that practice by using the course of posts as instructed, varying your pattern by weaving among them in a way that gives the fullest opportunities for your dog to grow lax and make a mistake. Include about five minutes of such work as part of each training session.

Occasionally there is a "geared" dog who is so insensitive to touch that he w'll consistently forge ahead as though immune to the effects of a hard-thrusting left knee, but who will respond to a device of logic. Simply walk with your dog at heel and, at an opportune time, close your eyes and turn left so that a bonafide accident causes you to fall over him. This casual approach seems so unplanned that a hyper-competitive dog will often accept it as a reason to stay out of the way of such an accident-prone slob.

Correcting or lessening the "geared" quality is one of the most difficult jobs in dog training. You will probably need to use all of the above techniques and lots of determined physical effort to succeed. Work until your dog has been thoroughly convinced that every distraction that occurs when he's heeling on leash has been planted to con him out in front of you. When he takes even an errant butterfly or a scented breeze as another reason to hold his position, you will be ready for the bridging link that will carry his attitude to the HEEL FREE. This link, and the method of attaching and using it, is described on pages 95 and 96, dealing with the lagging dog. Make any changes in the length and strength that are necessary to give surprise corrections that duplicate those you gave with the leash.

Slow Starts and Lagging

Whether a dog's lagging is caused by sluggishness, poor training methods or lack of sufficient work, the fault almost always takes the same pattern. On leash the dog generally walks as fast as his handler, but as far behind as he calculates can be done without the collar tightening, and comes ambling up to sit in position when the handler stops. He is apt to lag a bit farther behind on the FREE HEEL but, as on leash, comes up into position on the stops. The fault is costly in the ring, and is too embarrassing to condone.

Lagging on the Figure Eight

It is the necessity to eliminate lagging on the figure eight that has generated the most effective way of correcting the fault in all areas of free heeling. We employ the method religiously during the first few weeks of our Open Classes, and in the area of the figure eight where the trainer's hand is forced, no failures have been observed. Arrange for two helpers to serve as posts for a figure eight. If your dog is large, it is advised that the men wear work pants. For training purposes the posts should face each other with about ten feet between them.

With your dog on leash, position yourself to start the exercises just as you do in Novice work. Have one of the posts give you a forward command, then start to your left into the figure eight pattern. Walk at your normal gait with a bit more than the usual slack in the leash. Keep walking and hoping that your dog will lag as he generally does. *Slow down, if you must, to keep the full slack in the leash.* At the moment when his lagging behind you has placed him on the opposite side of the post to your left, lunge into a trot that jerks him into the post's leg. Keep moving forward until he's trapped so solidly behind the post that movement is impossible. Give him a few gasping moments to reflect on the horrors that his lagging brought, then lessen the angle of pull until he comes grating out from behind the post's legs.

84

When his lagging places him in a vulnerable position, run fast and trap him on a post. Study Page 84.

Start out again and hope fervently that he slumps into his usual lagging interval. Work until you trap him again. About the third time you try to booby-trap him you might find that he's working just as hard to stay on the same side of the post as you are, which means that he's up in good heel position. Rarely is it possible to trap a dog more than three times consecutively.

When your dog has reacted in the above way, you'll be prepared to give him experience in heeling while you trot rapidly through the figure eight pattern at least ten times a day for at least a month. *During this period, do not attempt the exercise with the dog off the leash.*

After the above amount of practice, you'll get the feeling that it would be impossible to run through a figure eight fast enough to foul your dog on a post. For the clincher, give him two weeks of work with the bridging link, using the techniques described on page 94. Then he'll be ready to FREE HEEL at your side, no matter how fast you walk through the figure eight.

Lagging on the Starts and the Straight Away

In the middle of your work area place something that will be a strong distraction to your dog. An aggressive cat in a cage or a staked-out chicken are examples of easily obtainable animate things. A plate of meat scraps could be used for a tempting sight or scent.

Bring the dog to the area at heel, and, holding only the hand loop of the leash, give him an "Okay" release. Saunter close to the distraction with a casual attitude that will cause him to feel completely free of command. When he's really involved with the sight, smell or sound, ease up close enough behind him to gain the proper slack for heeling, stealthily turn around, lock your hand tightly to your body and as you give a HEEL command start away at a trot. *Don't look back or make an argument out of your decision by arm-horsing him.* Such contention only makes the fault worse.

Don't be concerned because there was no interval between the command and your movement. If the dog reacted the instant he heard you, the slack would have given him time to respond before the leash tightened.

At this point, memory of your previous start may cause him to regard the distraction as another one of those situations which his novice work taught him to suspect. You might have to do a lot of relaxing before he lets himself get involved with the distraction again. If a few minutes of opportunity won't pull his mind from you, set up another distraction. Eventually he'll be tempted enough for you to demand another instant response to your HEEL command. Trot along for about ten feet, then terminate the exercise just as before.

Repeat this procedure until your command causes him to whirl from the distraction and into the HEEL position before the leash can tighten. Without slowing down, praise him for his alertness. End the period by taking him from the area and releasing him back to his own leisure—a "soaking time" which for an hour should not be interrupted by anyone. Four of such sessions will probably bring your dog to a point where you can make a change in your technique.

By now it's likely that he'll be hanging back against the leash in his reluctance to approach your distractions. If he wants to stay away, he'll want to go away. Fine! Do an about turn and "go away" very fast. You're not only letting him have his own way—you're helping him to it. He cannot want to start both fast and slow at the same time. But if he gambled that your start would be slowed—as usual—to accommodate his own descision, he got a rude jolt as your heavy momentum slugged into the leash. Regardless of his reaction to your start, move along at faster than normal speed for about twenty feet, then stop. When he sits automatically, praise him and let the slack out as you give him another, "Okay." Saunter back to the distraction in the most relaxed manner possible so that your dog will have the opportunity to become involved again.

The rebound from distraction, your command, and the fast start will soon become so strongly associated in the dog's mind that the full impetus will carry over to fast starts without the cue of tempting objects. This is true even with the classic slug and the dog that's been made contentious by arm-horsing.

Practice on the figure eight as described on page 84 and work around the heeling posts as explained in the part on the geared dog, as well as an occasional encounter with a single post, will give your dog added incentive to stay up in position. In such situations, of course, you will be moving ahead without tightening the leash to trap a dog that lags behind, instead of maneuvering him out in front of you as is done with the dog that forges ahead.

Changing pace to a trot from both the normal and slower gaits can be helpful at moments when a dog is lagging on a slack leash, and if it is done without looking back and arm-horsing. Keep your leash locked to your navel area and let your body weight give the jerk. There's no argument involved. You're simply going faster—with his head.

The question is often asked, and not illogically, whether coaxing could be used to get an otherwise reliable dog over his lagging, especially if he is soft or seems confused or intimidated by any pressure. It's true that "cookie trainers" have often bribed and baited dogs into rote patterns that have produced high scores in obedience competition. These "routine" dogs like most other "trick" dogs demonstrate the weakness of their motivation whenever they are faced with demands that are foreign to their patterns or temptations that are stronger than the bribes that conditioned them. With dogs as with humans, bribery is of doubtful value in establishing control and developing character. *Bribing a dog in one area will increase his resistance to positive methods in another.*

Better by far is obedience training that employs Nature's formula of necessity and reward. Of the two factors, necessity contributes the most to reliable performance. Praise your dog enthusiastically when he reacts favorably to your training, but don't let your praise deteriorate into coaxing. Soon he'll come to regard all situations, with or without distractions, as places to be in the heel position before the leash can tighten.

"But we're preparing for the HEEL FREE, so what about the fast starts and heeling off-leash?"

You'll find your answers in the part on the bridging link, page 93.

Sloppy or Lagging Turns

In novice classes, there is a great deal of interest among the spectators as they watch dogs, previously lagging on the right and about turns, begin to change with from less than thirty seconds of exposure to a simple sharpening technique. It can cure your dog of rounding off his corners or lagging in following your change of direction.

Move along with your dog at heel at a normal gait as you provide a bit more than the usual amount of slack and lock your leash hand tightly against your body. Without any preliminary to cue the dog, pivot sharply to the right and explode into two running steps, then settle back to a normal gait. Walk for a short distance, then repeat the pattern. By the third turn, if your lunging steps were explosive enough, you will find that your dog made a corner that was square and too fast for the leash to tighten.

Employ the same principle of impersonal necessity as you make about turns. Have sufficient slack, lock your hand to you, and, as you pivot, take two lunging steps in the new direction. Then return to a normal gait.

After you've made a few of both kinds of accelerated turns, you can perform a little experiment that will show you why bystanders are so amused. Simply follow the series of accelerated turns with some made at a normal speed. Quite a surprise? The same dog that may have shrugged off thousands of tugging, personal, "teaching" turns has within seconds accepted the lesson of impersonal physical necessity. Remember, the normal turns were but a brief interlude to evaluate your progress. Make a dozen training turns a day until sharpness has become your dog's way of heeling. Make an equal number using the bridging link according to the instructions beginning on page 93.

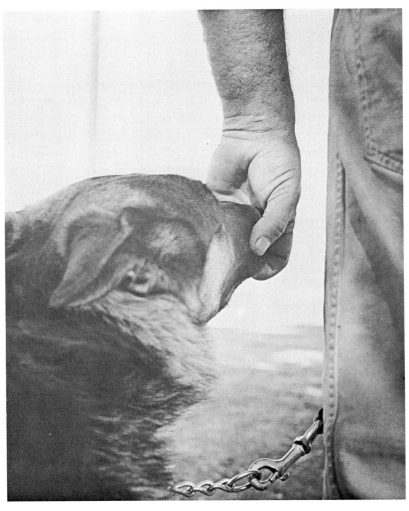

Nuzzling by a dog at heel can be stopped by grabbing and holding the offending nose.

Contact While Heeling and Sitting

The truth of the statement that "most of a dog's faults are due to his trainer" is seldom more evident than in the area of contact on the HEEL exercises. Here are some of the most common faults:

(1) Insufficient work on left turns.

(2) Tentative handling which prompts the dog to press against the handler for security.

(3) A desire to read the handler's moves through touch rather than by watching.

(4) Inattentiveness that would cause a dog to flounder into his handler or anything else in his path.

(5) Excessive and poorly-timed fondling by the handler which encourages the dog to make contact instead of avoiding it.

Whatever the cause, the best means of correcting the fault is the effective use of left turns, most of them of ninety degrees, and a sprinkling of forty-five degree turns which you can sneak into without the pause in forward motion which forewarns of a full left turn. This procedure will keep your dog guessing a bit.

It is surprising to see how often a dog who will shrug off the discomfort of sharply coordinated left turns will be impressed by an uncoordinated turn that is staged by the handler closing his eyes and turning left. It might be that one of these accidents where the handler falls over him or steps on a foot has a bonafide quality that leaves a bull-headed dog with nothing to contend against. The process is worth your try.

Leaning on the SIT

You can quickly discourage the leaner by making the right kinds of stops and starts. Stop with your left leg angled well back, which means that it will be behind the dog when he leans against you. When he has leaned, give a HEEL command and start with an emphasis that will convince the dog that leaning puts his rear in a very vulnerable position. He'll soon concentrate on staying out of the path of your left leg.

The bridging link.

Foot Contact

The dog who finishes an automatic SIT by putting his foot on that of the handler does so because he would rather keep contact through touching than by watching. You can stop this game of "top foot" by moving your foot just ahead of his touch and then coming down with just enough sole pressure to make him feel trapped.

Nudging and Nuzzling

These two faults in a dog's heeling and sitting are generally caused by a handler's own teddy bear complex or insecurity. There's a time for a good wholesome pat. There's no time for the fluttering, "Steady, boy," kitchy-koo that diverts a dog's mind from the elementary exercises of heeling and sitting. When your dog's nose comes close to your hand for the touching and fondling, "un-fondle" him by grasping the ball of his nose and trapping it tightly for about a minute. You must be consistent in your reaction if you are to stop your dog from nuzzling when he should be working.

The Bridging Link

Warning: Do not make this transition to the cord before the dog is working without contention in every conceivable situation on leash.

The dog who starts promptly and heels sharply lest he be caught flat-footed by the leash, only to backslide when the leash comes off, can be surprised and converted by the use of a simple device. This bridge from on-leash to off-leash accuracy can be a piece of shoemaker's thread or any of the new lines that are as strong and no heavier. Such a light weight will be almost unnoticeable to the Toy breeds and strong enough for a big dog. Regardless of his size, no dog *properly prepared* for this level of training will break such a line, or even argue with it.

Before you bring the dog into the area, set up a distraction.

93

Rigging the Line

Cut a piece of the bridging string about one foot shorter than your leash. Tie an end to the pull ring of the collar and the other end to the base rings as pictured on page 92. There is a good reason why we don't conveniently hook a loop to the snap—the thin material would slip out from under the latch. Hold the leash grip and the fold of line as shown in the picture.

Work the dog in the heeling exercise just as you've been doing, adding a few accelerated turns to make the dog doubly aware of the leash. When he's responding nicely, stop near the distractions and give him some praise. Now unsnap the leash in an obvious manner, *But do not tighten the cord or otherwise draw his attention to it* as you change to the leash grip shown on page 95.

Do your best to relax yourself and your dog, taking care not to tighten the cord. At the moment when the absence of the leash and the situation make the dog feel that school's out, give a HEEL command, and start fast. If your dog starts slowly, he'll learn that something too light to feel can give him a jolt he can't anticipate.

For several weeks, alternate between working the dog on leash and using the bridging link as instructed. When he works as well on the line as on the leash, you can cut it so that a piece six inches long hangs from his collar. He'll soon tire of trying to guess its length, and work as reliably on the HEEL FREE as he does on leash.

The feeling of "freedom" can bring a big surprise.

In addition to the visible distractions, this area is covered with tempting scents.

4

The Drop-On-Recall

No one who has seen the DROP-ON-RECALL used to prevent the kindling of a dog fight, or has seen a dog dropped short of the path of a speeding car could doubt the value of an exercise that will stop and hold a dog at a distance. Any dove- or duck-hunter who is caught short of cover by an approaching flight of birds will tell you that the ability to drop and freeze his dog can stop a movement that might flare the birds out of range.

One of the most useful of obedience exercises, the DROP-ON-RECALL consists of several distinct controls that a handler demonstrates with a dog at a distance: first, unless he is already moving toward his handler, there is the recall that starts the dog in the right direction; second, there is the DOWN command that orders the dog to drop in a safe or convenient place; third, there is the responsibility that causes the dog to hold the DOWN position until told to move; fourth, there is another recall command that brings the dog to the handler when the need for holding the DOWN-STAY has passed.

This exercise will have no value unless your dog performs it reliably: In fact, dependency on unreliable performance could be a hazard. Reliability will be developed by a training program that has no holes in it. Carefully follow the instructions. Do not omit or abridge any objective or process.

This "step-in" blocks any forward movement.

Level 1—Objective: to teach the dog to go down on command with the handler facing him from one step away, and to hold until told to move.

Select a work area at least ten feet square where the surface is level and traction is good. You can use a lawn unless the grass is slippery.

Bring your dog into the area on leash. Place him on a SIT-STAY, and step out to face him from one moderate step away. Hold the leash in your left hand at waist level, with no more sag than is needed to keep it free of tension. Focus on the ground just below the dog's nose. As—*not before*—your right foot steps quickly toward your dog to block forward movement, give a command, "Joe, down!" and use your right hand to grab the leash in a downward sweep that forces his immediate response.

Now that he's down, you can release your short grip on his leash and use your right hand to give him a light pat that tells him he has pleased you, but don't give him the feeling that the exercise is finished. *If he should break, you must jerk him, without a word, back to position in the usual manner of correcting a broken STAY.*

With the hand-loop held in the left hand, move around behind him just as you do when returning to him on the novice DOWN-STAY exercise. Be quick to jerk him back to position if he breaks as you circle.

When you've come up into place on his right side, give him another little pat to show him you are pleased that he continues to hold, but be quick to correct if he breaks at this point. Finish the exercise with a HEEL command and one step forward. After he sits automatically, give him a bit more praise and an "Okay" release that tells him he's on his own.

Let's study a technically perfect bit of handling from the dog's point of view. Because the command was given as you were already moving toward him, and the step was so fast, there was no time for any confused response to cause the dog to move forward. The right hand's short grip on the leash and

99

its downward sweep, so like the early enforcement of the DOWN command, left no doubt of what you wanted. *The fact that your fast step ended with your leg planted down in front of him prevented any creep forward after he was down.* The short grip wouldn't let him detour around the leg. Then came a warm wave of praise that told him he had pleased you immensely. *The pattern of your handling, correcting when needed and ending with praise, made it plain that the holding part of the exercise should be regarded as a DOWN-STAY.*

Repeat without variation the format of work, exactly as it is presented above, ten times each day for one week.

As you try to improve your handling technique, you should guard against some of the mistakes that seem common to training on the DROP-ON-RECALL. First, there is a tendency to let the all-out physical exertion of that blocking step toward the dog harden your DOWN command into the sound of a rebuff. If your dog has worked properly during his novice training, you should have no difficulty giving firm commands and making steps that will not appear to be corrections. The second mistake is the inhibited handling of those who protest that: "But he was told to stay—then forced to go down." One holding such groundless concern is prone to handle with tentative probing movements that will of themselves generate confusion as to just what indefinite thing the trainer is trying to do. Think of the many times during training and work that a dog is required to change from one exercise to another when a superseding command is given. With decisive but articulate commands and handling, such changes do not cause confusion.

Trial percentages show that a verbal command is better than a signal on the DROP-ON-RECALL, so don't confuse your dog and develop poor handling habits by working on signals at the present time.

Do not begin the next lesson before your dog has been worked at least a week on the above pattern and until he goes down before the leash can actually tighten on your step in.

100

Level 2—Objectives: (A) to down instantly on command from a SIT-STAY position and hold until ordered to move and (B) to learn to down and hold from a standing position as responsively as he does from the SIT-STAY.

The work of the first week has probably made your dog so responsive to your step-in and command that he downs before your fastest moves can tighten the leash on him. *Do not make the mistake of believing that his reliable performance at this level justifies the risk of giving the verbal command without the step and leash follow-through.* The harm of such an omission at this level, which gives the dog an opportunity to make a slow response or move toward his handler, is often reflected in the gyrations seen near obedience rings. Here, peculiar handlers warm up their dogs for the DROP-ON-RECALL by foot-stomping, short rushes, scolding, and other threats which are evidently intended to influence a dog's later performance in the ring where none of those rituals are permitted, and where clean, confident handling must obtain response to a single command. Not permitted to stamp, stoop, or burp loudly, such a handler can only quaver a supplication and dig his fingernails into his palms as his dog, seeing none of the familiar signs, ignores the DOWN command and comes all the way in on a full RECALL, or starts a slow slink that settles into a crouch somewhere along the line, or possibly drops an arm's length from the handler, instead of at the point where the judge indicated he should. Pitiful! Ten entry fees later it will be no better.

In other respects, many of these handlers, who gyrate in training as a preparation for situations where they cannot gyrate, are normal human beings. That makes it difficult to understand why they train with motions and double commands that convince their dogs that prompt response to a single command will never be demanded.

Equally puzzling, but more costly, are the actions of a retriever owner who lashes a dog down with an excess of words because he's too practical to use a single formal command and then wonders why the dog will not down when a flight of birds leave no time for the usual tirade.

You can avoid making your dog unreliable and yourself ludicrous when handling on the DROP-ON-RECALL by continuing to follow through with that step-in and leash snatch which leaves no time for slow responses. So do give yourself the essential foundation by continuing to follow through even though your dog drops so fast that it seems the leash could never tighten. Later, when he's off leash and a long way from you, you'll be glad you did.

Start the session by dropping your dog from the SIT-STAY a few times. Then give him a short break while you do some thinking about an important position to your pattern of work. This book's explanations and your own experience have shown you why the best foundation came from starting as you did.

Your success has qualified you to start building on that foundation by teaching your dog to drop from a STAND-STAY. This is a necessary intermediate step to accustom the dog to going down when he's up on all fours in preparation for the more complex demands of dropping him while he's in motion. Further, it gives the essential practice in going down completely and cleanly without hanging up in a half-sit, half-down position.

Step 1

Drop the dog from the SIT-STAY a few times, using the step-in technique you have mastered. Then give him a few minutes of break time.

Step 2

Place your dog on a novice STAND-STAY. Face him from a step out in front. From this stage, step in to down the dog and circle back around him to end the exercise just as you did when downing him from the SIT-STAY. If he disobeys by going down before he's told or otherwise moves without a command, correct him just as you did when he broke the STAYS in novice work, and continue on to complete the pattern from where the disobedience occurred.

Here are the answers to two questions that might be in your mind: first, if your handling is smooth and precise, your dog will not be confused by being made to down from a STAND; second, the exercise will not make the dog less dependable on the STAND-FOR-EXAMINATION exercise.

Because the approach develops concentration, not habit, he will become more reliable on the STAND.

Work until your dog has performed the above pattern acceptably three times. Give him a short break before going to the next step.

Step 3

Do three successive one-minute SIT-STAYS, holding the leash just as you do when preparing to work on the DROP, but each time return without dropping him.

If he anticipates and goes down or breaks the STAY in any way before you return to move him, correct him with the usual jerk back to the SIT-STAY position. Let him have a short break.

Step 4

Do three complete STAND-FOR-EXAMINATION exercises on leash, including having him hold while someone approaches and touches him, and you return to complete the exercise in the usual manner.

By repeating the above order of DROPS and STAYS eight times during two daily sessions for seven days, you will reach the objectives of having your dog DROP from both the SIT and STAND before your step-in can tighten the leash, and of having him hold without a break on the STAYS.

HE'LL BE DOWNING WHEN YOU TELL HIM TO, BUT NOT BEFORE.

Then you and your dog will be ready for the change in environment which is the salient feature of the next level of training.

Level 3—Objective: to bring the dog to a point of instant response to the DROP command, regardless of environment, with the trainer standing motionless a leash-length away.

The advantage of choosing the battlefield or actually setting the stage for contention is particularly valuable at this level of work on the DROP-ON-RECALL where the follow-through will be omitted and the dog will have his first physical opportunity to refuse the DOWN command. If you have never contrived to make such generalship work for you, the experience will give you an exhilarating insight as to its significance in your future dog training.

Remember: The procedure has a greater value than merely accustoming the dog to distractions so that unusual distractions will no longer affect him. By staging strong distractions to such an extent that the dog will be stimulated to contend against your will in situations where your leash will enable you to correct, you will make it more certain that he will respond to your commands when he is off leash and at a distance.

Pictured on page 113 are examples of distractions that can be obtained anywhere in the country. Your ingenuity will turn up many others equally effective.

Set an object on each side and another behind the spot where you will put your dog, so that each will be about five feet from him. To have them closer to him would cause your dog to turn sideways in an honest attempt to avoid something that reminds him of what your past training has labeled detour, or taboo.

Bring your dog on leash toward the set-up. If he has had adequate elementary training, he shouldn't be distracted from doing such a fundamental exercise as heeling near distractions. But if his attention does wander, sneak to a stop and surprise him with a stiff correction for failing to sit automatically.

Position the dog among the distractions as shown in the picture. Work him in the same rotation of DOWNS and returns that you used at the previous level. Follow through the same way and demand the same prompt and accurate performance, regardless of any effects from the distractions. Your corrections and his response will be a routine matter.

By the time you've repeated the rotation a few times, the presence of the objects around him will be turning his mind to his responsibility rather than distracting him from it. After two daily sessions of work, more if necessary, using the above distractions and rotation, your dog should be so attentive to you that he appears oblivious to the objects. You are ready to take a step that will call for a lot of honesty, concentration and coordination on your part.

Place your dog on the SIT-STAY amid the distractions just as though you were going to start through the rotation of DROPS and STAYS in the usual way. Face him from a step away and hold the leash as you have been doing. Without making any movement or gesture, give a strong DOWN command. Habit may prompt you to step toward him, so concentrate on holding still. *Give the dog the responsibility of responding to the verbal command without any motion or cue to remind him.*

Prior to this, as he heard the DOWN command, he saw you stepping toward him, which left no time to hesitate if he was going to drop before the leash could tighten. To sum it up, the follow-through and the distractions you've set up hav brought him past the point of contention at the present lev Now, as you eliminate the follow-through, you must show h..n that instant response to command will be enforced even though you stand motionless as you say the word. This will be the time for that concentration, honesty and coordination mentioned above.

Because of the foundation you've built, it is likely that your dog will go down on command even though he sees no accompanying movement. If so, return to him and finish the exercise in the usual way.

If he holds when he hears the command, as though waiting

for your movement, move in a way that he will remember. Dive in, grab your leash hold, and give him a DOWN correction that packs a lot more shock than your follow-through, and which convinces him that it's much better to go down on command than to wait for a move that will bring him discomfort.

Oh! So your dog is real sharp and went down before you could get to him! Here's the answer: when you dive in, grab the leash so that you can handily raise his front end about half his height from the ground and then jerk him back down with a correction. This can be done whether you are working a Saint Bernard or a Chihuahua, and without confusion to the dog.

To let the dog take your movement as a cue to go down just ahead of the correction, or to creep forward a fraction of an inch without discomfort, would guarantee total disrespect later when he is off leash and at a distance from you.

Go no further in his training if you are prone to give him more of a cue than the one word of command, or more than an instant in which to respond, or to allow him to creep toward you. Such a deficiency would mean your dog would be better off without the kind of training you would give him.

When you have made the correction, continue on around him, correcting for any break of the STAY, and complete the exercise as usual.

The fact that you are fast and relentless in your corrections makes it possible that your dog could take the start of your return on the SIT-STAY and STAND-STAY exercises as a reason to drop even though no command to DOWN was given. *This is why it is so important that you follow an oblique "look away" method of starting your return to the dog, instead of appearing to bear down on him as you do when you correct.*

Go through your rotation of DROPS and STAYS five times each day for seven days, or for longer if necessary, so that your dog will hold the STAYS without breaking and yet go down from either position on a single command. This will mean you are qualified to start work dropping the dog when he is moving toward you.

106

Level 4—Objective: to teach the dog to drop and hold on a short RECALL

You used the "step-in and follow-through" to take the dog past contention on the drop from both the SIT and STAND positions; now you will find the procedure equally effective in making the dog solid on dropping part way to you on a short RECALL on leash. Short and on leash because only when the effect of your handling is immediate and precise can you expect to stop the dog's forward motion and drop him on the exact spot where he receives your command.

To try to down him at a greater distance, or off leash, would be to destroy the foundation you have built and bring great difficulties at a later date.

You are faced with the most critical progression in the teaching of the DROP-ON-RECALL, so study the following instructions, and walk through them in your mind, until you feel certain that your comprehension and coordination will be as good as you can make them.

Place your dog on a SIT-STAY and move a full leash length in front of him. Hold the leash in your left hand as you face the dog for a few moments. Then, without any body movement, call him. Without pulling on the leash, take up the slack in such a way that you will be ready if a correction is needed. When the dog reaches a point halfway to you, which would be about a step away, give a DOWN command and take that step-in and follow-through just as you did when starting him to drop on the previous positions. If the dog downed instantly on command, your step-in will have placed you where you can reach down to give him a pat and a word of praise. If he didn't respond properly, your stance will block his forward movement, and the follow-through with your short leash grip should develop into a sharp correction that snatches him to a DOWN position *exactly where he received your command.*

Whether he dropped voluntarily or was corrected, give him the pat and the praise, and complete the exercise by requiring him to hold while you circle around behind him and move him with a HEEL command and a step. As always, give him the opportunity to sit automatically before you praise him.

For the next three days, repeat the above process exactly as it is given at least ten times each day.

The part of the exercise where the dog drops and holds requires more and better training than needed for the last part where the dog is merely called from where he has dropped to the usual place in front of the handler. This is why you are advised to repeat the above process, which stresses the important part, and disregard the latter part until later.

The three days of practice on stepping toward the dog as you drop him part way to you should have taught him to drop before the leash could tighten. From this point on, give the DOWN command without any move or gesture. If your dog fails to respond, or responds improperly, correct with a jerk that snatches him into the DOWN position on the exact spot where he received the command. If he overshoots the spot where he received the command, jerk him back to it.

Don't repeat the word "Down," nor ease the dog gently into position.

Later, you won't be able to do any repeating or easing, so you will be wise to take the dog past contention while your leash and proximity give you the advantage.

Following are some suggestions that might serve as answers to questions which could have occurred to you:

(1) If you haven't time to use the dog's name before giving the DOWN command, you can omit its use until greater distance will permit you to use its attention-getting advantages.

(2) If your dog is large or fast, you might find it necessary to take one step backwards as you call him from the STAY, in order to have room to drop him a step out in front of you.

Your dog should have three days of this responding to a verbal command, during which time you will move toward him only to correct, never to cue. By the end of that period, he should hold a SIT-STAY with you a leash-length away, come toward you when he's called, down instantly on command, and hold while you circle around behind him and end the exercise with a HEEL command.

Level 5—Objective: to teach the dog to drop on a short RE-CALL and hold until given the command to resume his move to the handler

Place your dog on a SIT-STAY and face him from a leash-length away. Have him hold for about half a minute; then, moving nothing but your mouth unless a correction is necessary, call him and down him halfway to you. Stand motionless for a count of about five while he holds the DOWN, then call him in to sit in front of you. If he doesn't respond when you call him, bring him in with the leash in a way that shows him that it's all right to move, not as though you were correcting him. The first few times you call him from the DOWN he might feel a bit confused, remembering the corrections he received whenever he moved before you returned to finish the exercise. Whether he responds to your command or is brought in with the leash, praise him in a way that tells him that the final result was just what you wanted. After he has been praised for doing a few RECALLS from where he downed, your dog might show a tendency to anticipate by coming in before he is called. *You must snuff out that anticipation by making a correction that snatches him back to a DOWN exactly where he was when he broke.*

"Snatch a Saint Bernard?" you might be asking. Certainly. You can make him so uncomfortable with a series of jerks that he will conclude it's best to stay on the DOWN until called.

After making the correction, go back and face him again from the spot where you stood. When he has held for a few seconds, return to him and finish the exercise as you did at the previous level. Returning in this way will show him that his drop won't always be followed by another RECALL.

You can do much to forestall confusion and anticipation if you will practice this simple formula:

Step 1

For five consecutive times have your dog hold a SIT-STAY a leash-length distant, come toward you when called, drop part way to you and hold that position until you call him to you. Give him a short break when you finish the exercise.

Step 2

Follow this by giving him five consecutive experiences in which you proceed just as is recommended above until the point where you have dropped him, but then instead of calling him to you, have him hold where he dropped until you return and end the exercise with a HEEL command. Give him another few minutes of break time.

Step 3

Provide five consecutive experiences in which the dogs holds the SIT-STAY until called and then comes directly to a SIT position in front of the handler.

The three exercises should be done only on leash so that you can make the proper correction promptly and effectively if your dog breaks a STAY or fails to respond to a command.

Go through the formula each day, putting more work on any parts where you feel your dog is below par. Within ten days it will be time to test your dog to see whether he needs more work before going on to the next level of training.

To test your dog, arrange distractions as you have done before. While your dog is exposed to their influence work him once on each of the three exercises in the practice formula. He should perform without contention.

Do not attempt the next level of training until your dog passes the test.

Level 6—Objective: performance on the longe of those objectives given for Level 5

The last lesson, through a variety of practice patterns, taught your dog to come toward you, drop halfway to you and then come on the last part of the RECALL, but to do no part of the exercise until he is given the proper command. Now, provided that you retain a means of making an immediate correction, it is reasonable to work for the same performance at a greater distance. Your fifteen-foot longe line will provide the right distance and the means of correction.

Use the longe to follow exactly each technique and progression in the order that was given for working with the leash. Although you've just finished Level 5, don't try to retrace the procedure by memory: you would be almost certain to forget some element. Review the lesson carefully.

There is another precaution you should take. When you face your dog a longe-length away or command him to drop half that distance to you, you'll need to remember the exact place where he receives the commands so that any corrections needed can be related to where the disobedience occurred. Don't ever correct your dog back to the wrong place.

You might need to work a few days longer with the longe line than you did with the leash before your dog will perform the work patterns as well as he did over the shorter distances. However, with enough effort, you can teach him that your demands can be enforced as inevitably, if not as promptly, as if he were on the leash.

Work your dog among distractions just as you did for the last lesson. Training classes in OPEN work can profit by mocking up an obedience ring, and working among the sights, sounds and smells of an improvised trial situation. Later, the dogs come to regard such a show-like atmosphere as a place where attention and quick response are demanded.

Your dog should do the work patterns on the longe without contention before you begin Level 7.

Level 7—Objective: reliable performance on a light line in preparation for off-line control

This lesson explains the work you will do on the line in preparation for the dog's dependable performance when he is at liberty. The procedure will require your utmost in concentration, ingenuity and honest effort.

Look at the picture on page 113. It shows the equipment you will need, and how it is fastened to the collar. The line is 100 feet and is made of ⅛ inch nylon, which is strong enough for the biggest dog, yet so light that he won't feel its length. Smaller nylon cords such as "mason's" line, obtainable at any hardware store, are better for small dogs. The tab that links the line to the collar is made of the same material as your fifteen-foot longe line. It extends about eight inches from the collar ring when made up and looped as shown. For small dogs, it should be taped so there is no gap to catch on his feet. A light but tough glove will protect your hands from cuts and burns. You will see why this simple equipment will make it possible for you to convince your dog that it would be well for him to obey your command without contention, even when he is at a distance and even though he feels no physical contact with you.

Take your dog to the training area, on leash, then equip him with the line and tab. See that there is slack in the line and that it is lying in loose skeins so that bunches of it will not act as a drag which would discourage the dog from disobeying, thus depriving you of the opportunity for a surprise correction.

It would be good if he were to forget all about the line, so don't hold on to it. If you can't pounce onto one hundred feet of line before the dog can run away, you don't have what it takes to train him.

Leave the dog and face him from about twenty feet away. Work him in the same patterns you used when he was on the leash and longe. Hopefully, the greater distance will cause him to disobey some part of the exercise and give you the opportunity for correction, but it might be that the weight of the

Light line work amid distractions builds reliability.

tab will give him the feeling that you might not be as help-less as the greater distances would suggest. If such is the case, you may have to work quite a while before you get your first chance to correct.

It is unlikely at this stage of training that your dog will try to run away to avoid correction, but if he does, jump on the line and grab with your gloved hand. Work your way down the line to a good hand-hold on the tab and correct just as you would with a short grip on a leash or longe. Don't feel that you are less effective because it requires a lot of reeling and maneuvering before you get to the tab. From the foundation you've given him, your dog knows exactly what he's supposed to do; so, no matter how late it comes, make that correction a stiff one. Later, when your dog is off leash, you both might have to pay for any inhibited corrections you give now.

Before you bring the dog into the area to start the second day's work, lay the line so that at least twenty-five feet of it run straight away from where you plan to start the dog work-ing. Next, bring the dog into the area with the tab on the collar and attach the line.

Leave the dog on a SIT-STAY and follow the line out about forty feet before you turn to face him. Give him some experi-ence in dropping halfway to you, being sure to mark the spots where he should respond to command so that you can correct him back to the right place. If you think this emphasis on the right place is superfluous when working on these long dis-tances, consider the experienced bird-dog trainer who, when steadying a pointer, will throw his hat down to mark a spot where a broken point occurred and bring the offending dog back to that place from as much as a quarter of a mile away.

Work until the dog is dropping reliably at the above dis-tance, then put him away for the day.

On the following day, plant some distractions in the area and work the dog among them on the above exercise. By now you are certainly aware that one of the strongest forces in dog training is that of exposing a dog to more and stronger dis-tractions, when you have a means of enforcing your commands, than he would encounter by chance when you have no physical controls. If your dog's early training followed a logical vein, you have used the principle many times. Use it now against the time when you might be called upon to save your dog's life by stopping and holding him under strange and dangerous conditions.

Here are a few emergencies to add to the things you have in mind:

Have someone suddenly appear and run by him with another dog just as you give your DOWN command. Give him a lot of line work close to the movement and sound of traffic. Practice bringing him in from the forty-foot distance and dropping him beside some good smells that you've planted.

Again, the effectiveness of your correction need not be lost just because of the time needed to work your way down the line to a hand-hold on the tab. If you feel that the distance from the dog and the difficult handling of the line would prompt him to make an all-out attack on a distraction, you have done a poor job of basic training and neither you nor your dog are ready for OPEN work.

Whether it takes ten minutes or a long time, work until your dog is past contention around the distractions, then quit for the day.

You have probably been concerned with the fact that the need for the DROP-ON-RECALL is not so likely to occur when a dog is holding a STAY as when he is moving about his own affairs as a free agent. True. The patterns you have been using give the controlled situations necessary to teach and perfect the exercise, but now we'll begin to adapt the controls to the most practical uses.

Take the dog to an interesting area where both of you will enjoy walking. Equip him with the line and tab. Give him an "Okay" release and by your attitude encourage him to enjoy himself in his own way. It might be that your work with leash, longe and line has so impressed him that his attention will leave you only in short spans. If so, congratulations. Such attentiveness will be invaluable later when he's at liberty. You may have to enjoy yourselves quite a while before he'll loosen up enough to become engrossed in the sights and smells around him. Whatever the attraction, let his interest develop fully, then, regardless of how far he is from you, call him and after he's moved a few feet toward you give him a DOWN command. If he drops, go to him with a lot of praise. Be just as emphatic with your correction if it is needed.

Whether your dog dropped willingly or was corrected, finish the exercise by walking around behind him and into a position that puts him on your left side. Heel him out of the DOWN, then tell him "Okay," and let him go back to enjoying the sights and smells the area affords. Work for whatever time you can spare at the relaxed procedure of letting the dog get involved with an attraction and then stopping his movement by dropping him.

This can be before he has a chance to start toward you, as well as on RECALLS.

When he is working reliably under all types of conditions, you can call him in from where you drop him, and finish the exercise as you would any RECALL. But vary the procedure occasionally by going to where he has dropped and heeling him off from the spot. This will prevent the last part of the exercise from becoming habit instead of response to command.

Work as instructed with the line and tab until your dog drops reliably on command in all situations at distances up to seventy-five feet. Then work until he shows the same reliability when he is equipped with nothing more than a tab. Only then is it advisable to do the exercise when the dog wears no handle for you to grip.

In the supplementary sections that apply to areas of specific need, you will find further suggestions for increasing your dog's reliability.

The DROP-ON-RECALL will save you much inconvenience. It could save your dog's life.

The Drop On Recall can save your dog's life.

5

The Broad Jump

EXPERIENCED class instructors in all parts of the country have watched their students work hard and successfully on what are commonly thought to be the most difficult exercises in OPEN work and then become horribly snagged on what was casually approached as the simple BROAD JUMP. The fault most common to the exercise is that of a dog walking the boards with the ritualistic dedication of a Fiji firewalker crossing hot stones. A great variety of ingenious devices have sprung from the premise that if the boards are uncomfortable enough the dog will see the advantage of being airborne when he crosses them. Without doubt such aids can help prevent the walking fault, particularly in combination with another asset.

Since 1946 the classes of the Orange Empire Dog Club have been an excellent proving ground for training methods. Our efforts have found no reasonable alternative to teaching the BROAD JUMP with a series of progressions that allow no time for walking.

Begin the first period by placing the highest of the four jumps, or whatever substitute you might start with, where you will have at least thirty feet of good running surface when approaching and leaving it, so that you and the dog can jump and land with good traction.

Broad jumps can be equipped with wire jackets that will cause discomfort but not injury.

With the dog on the leash, line up on the center of the jump from about twenty feet away. Hold the leash in your left hand with the slack reduced so that the dog cannot avoid the jump when you go over it. Give a HEEL command and run—don't walk—toward the center of the jump. Your alignment and short leash will make it impossible for him to avoid the jump. When it is imminent, command, "Joe, over!" Upon landing, give a bit of praise, and walk back to position for another run at the jump. Until told to do differently, don't vary the pattern of the fast approach, jump, and praise. Unfortunately, a handler will sometimes decide that his dog is exceptional and should be treated as such when after only a half-dozen jumps the dog's enthusiasm is fired to where he is rushing to take the jump with wild abandon. The trainer slows down or otherwise varies the pattern, which allows the dog to make a mistake that is very difficult to correct. Avoid such a mistake.

Ten times over the jump is enough for the first lesson. An equal number of sessions each day for a week will convince your dog that the only way across the board is to jump, and that any attempt to detour will come up against the leash and your momentum.

After the first week's work, it will be time to establish the distance that your dog must jump in the ring, so that you can start to gradually familiarize him with future demands. The American Kennel Club's requirement is that a dog broad jump a distance that is double the height he is required to clear in the RETRIEVE OVER THE HIGH JUMP exercise (see page 70).

Those figures set forth the requirements but they do not indicate a very important fact. The trainer of a tiny dog often has the biggest problem in progressively working toward the full distance his dog must jump. For example, a Chihuahua eight inches tall at the shoulder should clear an obstacle twelve inches high and broad-jump a distance of 24 inches, which is no great physical task but does pose a problem which can only be appreciated when seen from the dog's point of view. Place regulation jumps for such a dog, then lie down and look from

"Run!"

the level where the dog's eyes would be at the point where he would be placed for the jump.

"What jump?" you might ask. You're looking at what appears to be a solid platform with the space between the boards not apparent from the dog's viewpoint. From this perspective, you will see why it is especially important to put the wire or other bad footing in place when you add the second board.

Regulations give the handler a choice of using a lesser number of boards in cases where the required distance would crowd a greater number into an almost solid platform. So do some looking and thinking on the subject. Do not add more boards or distance than you yourself can jump until the dog is so deeply in the groove that the sight of the BROAD JUMP is a synonym for "Over."

When you reach a point where the dog goes over the jumps with you without the slightest hesitancy or swerving, you can make a bit of a change. Align your approach runs so that your own path will be close along the right hand side of the jumps. Extend your arm so that your dog will be forced to jump the boards in association with your "Joe, over" command. As you pass the last board, veer to the left about two feet to keep any difference in your relative speeds from pulling the dog's alignment from the jump and to lay the groundwork for the next progression.

It is at this level, where you have the advantage of your swift run beside the jumps, that you should gradually add boards and distance to equal what your dog must jump in the ring.

The jumping can well be done in several daily periods interset with other exercises. *Do not try to jump your dog off leash or at a slower speed.*

Four weeks of jumping the dog as you run beside the boards should find him performing as certainly as when you jumped with him. It will then be time for the next progression.

You will only understand the importance of the next step if you review how the jumping pattern has developed thus far.

At the first level the speed and alignment of your run forced the dog to jump the boards. At the second level his foundation, combined with your handling of the leash as you ran close to the boards, caused him to jump. You can well believe that the transition from the run to the command that is given without any motion is a key step in teaching the exercise. It will require the utmost in your technique and timing.

Place your dog on a SIT-STAY facing the jumps as close as you feel he can be without restricting his front action when jumping. Hold the leash in your left hand with the arm fully extended toward the dog, so that the leash won't tighten as you move around to take a position beside the jumps. This extension of arm and leash should position you so that you face the last board with your toes a foot from it. If the spread of your dog's placement and the distance he must jump is more than the leash and your arm will span, adjust the boards or remove one of them, and use the shorter distance until told otherwise.

Possibly, in gauging the leash length and lining up with the jumps, your actions have influenced the dog to break his STAY. If so, make a correction that will convince him he should move only on command. He should not only hold to qualify in the ring, but it would be impossible to work him properly on the jumps in training unless he is solid on his STAYS. Double check to see that you and the dog are in good relationship with the jumps, and that the leash is correctly held.

Command "Over," and as you do—*not after,* turn and lunge at an angle toward a spot about a foot in front of where you calculate the jumping dog will land; then turn and run squarely away from the jumps as though you had actually jumped them.

If your handling was adequate, this is what happened to the dog: your firm command, coordinated with the fast start, made it clear that he had better jump the instant he got your command. If he hesitated or tried to detour around the jump, the force and angle of your run propelled him over, convincing him that just because you stood quietly was no reason to believe that you would remain that way. In short, your ex-

Start of the "breakaway."

The "breakaway."

plosive starts will tell him that it is better to jump when he hears the word than to sit until he sees you move.

If the dog came around the jump, stepped on a board, or outmaneuvered you in some other way, recheck everything from your relative positions through the angle of your run. When the pattern is right, you'll get the results described above. Work your dog on six of these patterns every day, interspering them with other exercises.

Generally, if a dog has a good foundation, ten days of these patterns will take him to the point where he holds the STAY until he gets your command and clears the jumps before your run can tighten the leash. But use any extra time necessary to take him past contention at this level before you go to the next step.

This preparation should include some additional work with the longe line if your dog's size forced you to do the previous leash exercise with the boards set at less distance than will be required in the ring. Now that good solid leash work has the dog past contention, you can use your longe to hold the dog in the same pattern as you gradually work toward placing and jumping him as you will when he's working in the ring.

Whether your dog is big enough to require work with the longe line or is small enough to need only the leash, begin to extend the pattern until he is jumping about 10% further than he'll have to in the ring, so that he'll be conditioned to put forth more than the minimum necessary effort. When you reach the point where the dog jumps that distance before your run can tighten the leash, you'll be prepared to start the next step.

Begin this level by placing the dog on STAY before the jumps and taking a position beside the jumps, the leash or longe held in your extended hand, just as you did on the previous exercises. After he has held for four or five seconds, give the "Over" command. *Stand motionless until your dog has left the ground,* then turn and make your follow-through beside the jumps so that you will join the dog when he lands in much the same relationship as if you had jumped the

126

boards with him. This will give him more reason to feel it is wise to make a good all-out jump on command and not cut corners. Work for as many periods as are needed to convince you that making clean jumps on command has become a way of life with your dog. Then go to the next level.

For many days your dog has been solid on his STAY before the jumps, and has jumped infallibly on command. Your runs have not been a cue, but have been follow-throughs that have confirmed his judgment. You and your dog are prepared to start the final part of the BROAD JUMP exercise, wherein the handler executes a simple right-face while the jumping dog is in the air, then stands motionless while the dog lands and turns right to double back to sit before him. After he receives the finish command, the dog completes the exercise by going to the HEEL position. The mechanics of teaching this final step are simple, but you must work carefully to avoid confusing the dog.

First you must decide whether your dog is so big or such an exceptional jumper that you must use the longe instead of the leash. There must be no chance that the dog will accidentally be jerked up short. Next, place the dog for the jump in the usual way. Stand facing the jumps from a position of your choice which, as the rules specify, can be anywhere within the range of the first and last boards, with your toes about two feet back from the boards. Command, "Joe, over." When the dog's hind feet leave the ground, do a right face and extend your arm so that there will be enough slack when he lands to prevent a discouraging jerk. Now, without moving from where you stand, gently use the leash or line to give what encouragement is necessary to turn the dog around to his right and bring him to a SIT in front of you. Most dogs seem to do that part of the exercise almost instinctively.

Do not call the dog to you—it is not a RECALL.

Whether he comes and sits in front of you of his own initiative or needs the leash cue persuasion, convince him with praise that he's the world's greatest dog. End the exercise by having him finish.

Even though your dog did the complete BROAD JUMP exercise flawlessly, put down any temptation to try him off the line. As you work at tidying up the dog's performance, you'll have need for physical control. While you are polishing, make sure you are consistent in placing him in the best possible position to take off for his jump. Often a dog is handicapped by starting the exercise in improper relation to the boards.

Condition him to wait for your command before he jumps by occasionally having him hold a SIT-STAY longer than usual and then return to heel him off with jumping him.

If it is needed, you can correct the inaccuracies on the "sit in front and finish" with the same mechanics you used on the novice RECALL work.

Practice for enough days to bring the feeling that your dog is completely past contention on the exercise; then challenge his reliability by working him around distracting conditions. When he does the exercise regardless of his environment, work him with a line so light that its weight is unnoticeable but strong enough to give a surprise correction. Even with the protection of a glove on your hand, the light line will not be as effective as the leash or longe, but a couple of surprises will convince the dog he should stay in the groove regardless of how free the line's lightness makes him feel.

After a few days of such practice, cut the line to his body length. Work him another few days with the short line dangling from his collar. *He won't look to see how long it is or whether you're holding its end.* Then you will be prepared to take the line off and work him just as you will be required to do in the ring.

Because your dog's concept of the exercise was built block by block, you probably won't be plagued with the board-walking and corner-cutting so often demonstrated by dogs that have been worked speculatively. Any difficulty you would experience is probably due to insufficient work with the line at one of the levels. Correction lies in retracing the line work until the dog is completely past contention around the strongest distractions.

After the jump, bring him in to you.

"The Ugly Dachshund" and his *"littermates"* on a stay.

6

The Stays

THE difference between NOVICE and OPEN STAY exercises is more than one of degree. Not only is the OPEN dog required to hold for longer periods, but he must do so with the handler out of sight, which demands a much higher level of responsibility.

It is not unusual for a person who has learned the effective ways of handling on the STAYS in NOVICE training to become careless or forgetful in OPEN work. A close check on handling habits is the first step toward OPEN responsibility.

How do you leave the dog? Do you remember to start on the right foot as you walk away from him? Through association, it can be part of a command to stay, just as stepping out on the left foot can add emphasis to your HEEL command.

Do you follow the procedure of circling around the dog counter-clockwise twice and standing motionless beside him for a half minute before you end the exercise with a HEEL command and one step forward? It is the best insurance against having a dog move from position before the judge says, "Exercise finished."

Another area to check for sloppy handling is that of correction. Handlers who should know better are guilty of such irrational actions as walking a dog back to where he broke a

STAY and then actually telling him to stay a second time, instead of correcting him all the way back from where he was apprehended in a way that tells him there will be no second command, only a correction if he breaks.

Be certain that you are doing a good job of handling before you start extending the dog with the situations described below.

The picture on page 133 shows how the corner of a building and some distractions are used to condition a dog to hold STAYS when the handler is out of sight. The second person in the background can give a signal if the dog tries to fudge toward a distraction or sniff the scents that have been placed just out of his stretching range. Two quick steps could bring the handler from his hiding place to make a correction that would show the dog he can appear from hiding almost instantly. A dog should have a great deal of this conditioning before he is worked where the handler cannot make this quick reappearance. Progressively extend the holding time until the dog will consistently hold seven minutes on the SIT-STAY and at least fifteen minutes on the DOWN-STAY. Then you'll be prepared to work him on the next level of STAYS while you are out of sight.

Create a ring atmosphere similar to the one pictured. In addition to the distractions that are visible, there are others, including small pieces of meat, and a variety of scents such as fox, muskrat and bear. See page 141 for information on obtaining scents.

Help your dog taste a bit of success by letting him earn praise for staying only a minute on each of the STAY exercises for the first few days that you work him in the loaded ring.

Be certain that your manner of returning to him to end the exercise does not resemble the rushes you make to correct, otherwise he might experience a few moments of confusion. Stroll back casually, without looking directly at him, and circle around him twice (in the way previously described) before you end the exercise, so that he will be conditioned to wait longer between your return and the end of the exer-

A good corner set-up.

cise than is required when you return to him in a trial. It is heartbreaking to have a dog blow his passing score in the last few seconds of a trial.

After a few days, gradually lengthen the STAY periods until he is holding about twice as long on the SIT-STAY and DOWN-STAY as he will need to in competition. If your handling is good and your distractions are varied and strong, he'll reach the point where unusual sights, sounds and smells will remind him of his responsibility instead of tempting him from it.

Working the dog on the STAY positions in the manner described above will do more than improve the dog's performance in the ring. Such practice can calm a nervous dog and make him a much more pleasant companion. Used with the exercises presented in the heeling section, it can be a big factor in stabilizing the "geared" dog described on page 78.

7

Polishing for Ring, Home and Field

Polishing for the Ring

The following four steps will help a handler make higher scores with his well-trained dog.

(1) Spend time at a couple of trials in studying the handling and judging in the class you will be entering. Make notes.

(2) Set up a practice ring like the one in the picture, and work your dog among the distractions progressively on the leash, longe line and light line until you feel that the dog will remember his responsibility regardless of what might occur in a trial.

(3) Have an experienced handler or judge direct you in the ring procedure as though you were participating in a trial, scoring a penalty for each mistake your dog makes.

(4) Continue to practice in your "loaded" ring and other places until you feel that you have brought your performance to the highest level.

Polishing for the Home

It is surprising how a capable handler will do such a masterful job of setting up distractions in training for obedience competition that the temptations of the ring are pale by comparison, and then fail to set up training situations in the area of companionship at home or on the street. In fact, some handlers only attempt to influence their dogs in good behavior when emergencies occur and they are unprepared to correct.

Obviously, this failure to get the fullest benefit from their dog's training is not due to lack of ability, but to lack of decision. Decide that your dog is going to respond as reliably in home life as he does in the ring. Then set up the training situations necessary to reach that objective.

Polishing for the Field

Volumes have been written about innumerable facets of training a retriever for land and water—in fact, about almost everything related to the training of a retriever except an inch-by-inch explanation of how to teach a dog to retrieve when he doesn't do so naturally or as a delightful game.

True, when they have finished describing the joys of the game most of them allow that hard mouths and other faults are most easily corrected in dogs that have been force-broken to retrieve. Can it be that their authors do not understand why the dog that has been trained by methodical, positive motivations is less likely to develop the mouthing fault than the dog who regards the whole thing as more of a romp than a responsibility?

A course in OPEN work plus a little extra experience on dummies and birds in the field environment will produce a usable dog that will continue to improve in his working relationship with his master. On the other hand, a dog who might be outstanding in natural ability, but who has never had the close orientation to his master that thorough obedience training gives, will continue to do things for himself alone because that is the attitude upon which his training was founded.

Don't be one of those unimaginative trainers who waits for the hunting season before practicing with his dog in environment that duplicates the physical situation where his dog will be used. Give your dog lots of practice on the DROP-ON-RECALL and on the STAYS while you are carrying a shotgun in what appears to the dog to be a hunting situation.

Don't worry that bearing down heavily on control will lessen his drive; you'll simply steer it in the right direction. Ask yourself how many times you've seen a hunter do a smooth job of correcting a sloppy dog when he's on one of his rare trips afield. Your answer to this question should indicate the importance of practice in the field.

There are many good dummies and small boat bumpers available at sporting goods stores, pet shops, and boat supply shops. They are ideally suited for practice in both cover and water, and a good preliminary step to the handling of birds. Use the same scent on your training dummy and pigeons as on the game you will eventually hunt in order to keep a continuity for the dog's nose through all of your polishing for the field.

The National Scent Company, 10660 Stanford Avenue, Garden Grove, California, makes a variety of scents, including pheasant, quail, partridge and duck. They are economical and easily applied.

An unfortunate experience, handler laxity, or an extreme change in environment could cause your dog to develop a fault in ring, home, or field. Obviously, careful consideration of all aspects of the fault and its origin should precede any attempts at correction. Next, duplicate the environment and the mechanical situation that existed when the fault first occurred; and, beginning at the level of the light line, work the dog among distractions that are stronger than any the dog has seen before. Continue the process until the dog is completely past contention and is enjoying praise for good performance. Do not limit your work to the specific problem exercise. Practice the other Open Exercises even though they might appear unrelated to the dog's fault. As in any kind of "patching," a big patch with lots of overlap makes the strongest mend.

Regulations for American Kennel Club Licensed Obedience Trials

(As in effect January 1, 1975)

Purpose

Obedience trials are a sport and all participants should be guided by the principles of good sportsmanship both in and outside of the ring. The purpose of obedience trials is to demonstrate the usefulness of the pure-bred dog as a companion of man, not merely the dog's ability to follow specified routines in the obedience ring. While all contestants in a class are required to perform the same exercises in substantially the same way so that the relative quality of the various performances may be compared and scored, the basic objective of obedience trials is to produce dogs that have been trained and conditioned always to behave in the home, in public places, and in the presence of other dogs, in a manner that will reflect credit on the sport of obedience. The performances of dog and handler in the ring must be accurate and correct and must conform to the requirements of these regulations. However, it is also essential that the dog demonstrate willingness and enjoyment of its work, and that smoothness and naturalness on the part of the handler be given precedence over a performance based on military precision and peremptory commands.

CHAPTER 1

General Regulations

Section 1. **Obedience Clubs.** An obedience club that meets all the requirements of The American Kennel Club and wishes to hold an Obedience Trial at which qualifying scores toward an obedience title may be awarded, must make application to The American Kennel Club on the form provided for permission to hold such trial. Such a trial, if approved, may be held either in conjunction with a dog show or as a separate event. If the club is not a member of The American Kennel Club it shall pay a license fee for the privilege of holding such trial, the amount of which shall be determined by the Board of Directors of The American Kennel Club. If the club fails to hold its trial at the time and place which have been approved, the amount of the license fee paid will be returned.

Section 2. **Dog Show and Specialty Clubs.** A dog show club may be granted permission to hold a licensed or member obedience trial at its dog show, and a specialty club may also be granted permission to hold a licensed or member obedience trial if, in the opinion of the Board of Directors of The American Kennel Club, such clubs are qualified to do so.

Section 3. **Obedience Classes.** A licensed or member obedience trial need not include all of the regular obedience classes defined in these Regulations, but a club will be approved to hold Open classes only if it also holds Novice classes, and a club will be approved to hold a Utility class only if it also holds Novice and Open classes. A specialty club which has been approved to hold a licensed or member obedience trial, if qualified in the opinion of the Board of Directors of The American Kennel Club, or an obedience club which has been approved to hold a licensed or member obedience trial may, subject to the approval of The American Kennel Club, offer additional nonregular classes for dogs not less than six months of age, provided a clear and complete description of the eligibility requirements and performance requirements for each such class appears in the premium list. However, the nonregular classes defined in these Regulations need not be described in the premium list. Pre-Novice classes will not be approved at licensed or member obedience trials.

Section 4. **Tracking Tests.** A club that has been approved to hold licensed or member obedience trials and that meets the requirements of The American Kennel Club, may also make application to hold a Tracking Test. A club may not hold a tracking test on the same day as its show or obedience trial, but the tracking test may be announced in the premium list for the show or trial, and the tracking test entries may be included in the show or obedience trial catalog. If the entries are not listed in the catalog for the show or obedience trial, the club must provide, at the tracking test, several copies of a sheet, which may be typewritten, giving all the information that would be contained in the catalog for each entered dog. If the tracking test is to be held within 7 days of the obedience trial the entries must be sent to the same person designated to receive the obedience trial entries, and the same closing date should apply. If the tracking test is not to be held within 7 days of the obedience trial the club may name someone else in the premium list to receive the tracking test entries, and may specify a different closing date for entries at least 7 days before the tracking test.

The presence of a veterinarian shall not be required at a tracking test.

Section 5. **Obedience Trial Committee.** If an obedience trial is held by an obedience club, an Obedience Trial Committee must be appointed by the club, and this committee shall exercise all the authority vested in a dog show's Bench Show Committee. If an obedience club holds its obedience trial in conjunction with a dog show, then the Obedience Trial Committee shall have sole jurisdiction only over those dogs entered in the obedience trial and their handlers and owners; provided, however, that if any dog is entered in both obedience and breed classes, then the Obedience Trial Committee shall have jurisdiction over such dog, its owner, and its handler, only in matters pertaining to the Obedience Regulations, and the Bench Show Committee shall have jurisdiction over such dog, its owner and handler, in all other matters.

When an obedience trial is to be held in conjunction with a dog show by the club which has been granted permission to hold the show, the club's Bench Show Committee shall include one person designated as "Obedience Chairman." At such event the Bench Show Committee of the show-giving club shall have sole jurisdiction over all matters which may properly come before it, regardless of whether the matter has to do with the dog show or with the obedience trial.

Section 6. **Sanctioned Matches.** A club may hold an Obedience Match by obtaining the sanction of The American Kennel Club. Sanctioned obedience matches shall be governed by such regulations as may be adopted by the Board of Directors of The American Kennel Club. Scores awarded at such matches will not be entered in the records of The American Kennel Club nor count towards an obedience title.

All of these Obedience Regulations shall also apply to sanctioned matches except for those sections in which it is specified that the provisions apply to licensed or member trials, and except where specifically stated otherwise in the Regulations for Sanctioned Matches.

140

Section 7. **American Kennel Club Sanction.** American Kennel Club sanction must be obtained by any club that holds American Kennel Club obedience trials, for any type of match for which it solicits or accepts entries from non-members.

Section 8. **Dog Show Rules.** All the Dog Show Rules, where applicable, shall govern the conduct of obedience trials and tracking tests, and shall apply to all persons and dogs participating in them except as these Obedience Regulations may provide otherwise.

Section 9. **Identification.** No badges, club jackets, coats with kennel names thereon or ribbon prizes shall be worn or displayed, nor other visible means of identification used, by an individual when exhibiting a dog in the ring.

Section 10. **Immediate Family.** As used in this chapter, "immediate family" means husband, wife, father, mother, son, daughter, brother, or sister.

Section 11. **Pure-Bred Dogs Only.** As used in these regulations the word "dog" refers to either sex but only to dogs that are pure-bred of a breed eligible for registration in the American Kennel Club stud book or for entry in the Miscellaneous Class at American Kennel Club dog shows, as only such dogs may compete in obedience trials, tracking tests, or sanctioned matches. A judge must report to The American Kennel Club after the trial or tracking test any dog shown under him which in his opinion appears not to be pure-bred.

Section 12. **Unregistered Dogs.** Chapter 16, Section 1 of the Dog Show Rules shall apply to entries in licensed or member obedience trials and tracking tests, except that an eligible unregistered dog for which an ILP number has been issued by The American Kennel Club may be entered indefinitely in such events provided the ILP number is shown on each entry form.

Section 13. **Dogs That May Not Compete.** No dog belonging wholly or in part to a judge or to a Show or Obedience Trial Secretary, Superintendent, or veterinarian, or to any member of such person's immediate family or household, shall be entered in any dog show, obedience trial, or tracking test at which such person officiates or is scheduled to officiate. This applies to both obedience and dog show judges when an obedience trial is held in conjunction with a dog show. However, a tracking test shall be considered a separate event for the purpose of this section.

No dogs shall be entered or shown under a judge at an obedience trial or tracking test if the dog has been owned, sold, held under lease, handled in the ring, boarded, or has been regularly trained or instructed, within one year prior to the date of the obedience trial or tracking test, by the judge or by any member of his immediate family or household, and no such dog shall be eligible to compete. "Trained or instructed" applies equally to judges who train professionally or as amateurs, and to judges who train individual dogs or who train or instruct dogs in classes with or through their handlers.

Section 14. **Qualifying Score.** A qualifying score shall be comprised of scores of more than 50% of the available points in each exercise and a final score of 170 or more points, earned in a single regular or nonregular class at a licensed or member Obedience Trial or Sanctioned Match.

Section 15. **When Titles Are Won.** Where any of the following sections of the regulations excludes from a particular obedience class dogs that have won a particular obedience title, eligibility to enter that class shall be determined as follows: a dog may continue to be shown in such a class after its handler has been notified by three different judges of regular classes in licensed or member trials, that it has received three qualifying scores for such title, but may not be entered or shown in such a class in any obedience trial of which the closing date for entries occurs after the owner has received official notification from The American Kennel Club that the dog has won the particular obedience title.

Where any of the following sections of the regulations require that a dog shall have won a particular obedience title before competing in a particular obedience class, a dog may not be shown in such class at any obedience trial before the owner has received official notification from The American Kennel Club that the dog has won the required title.

SUGGESTED CONSTRUCTION OF HIGH JUMP
FRONT VIEW OF HIGH JUMP

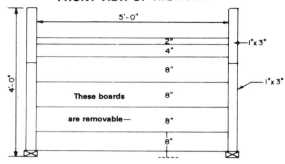

5'-0"

2"
4"
8"
8"
8"
8"

1"x 3"

1"x 3"

4'-0"

These boards

are removable—

SIDE VIEW OF HIGH JUMP

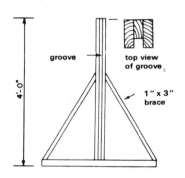

groove

top view
of groove

1" x 3"
brace

4'-0"

This upright consists of two pieces 1" x 3" and one piece 1" x 2", nailed together, with the 1" x 2" forming the groove for the boards to slide in.

The high jump must be painted a flat white.

SUGGESTED CONSTRUCTION OF BROAD JUMP

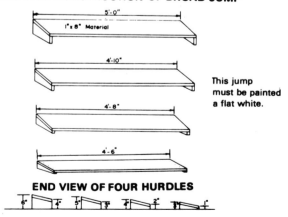

5'-0"
1" x 8" Material

4'-10"

4'-8"

4'-6"

This jump must be painted a flat white.

END VIEW OF FOUR HURDLES

6"   5"   4"   3"

SUGGESTED CONSTRUCTION
OF BAR JUMP

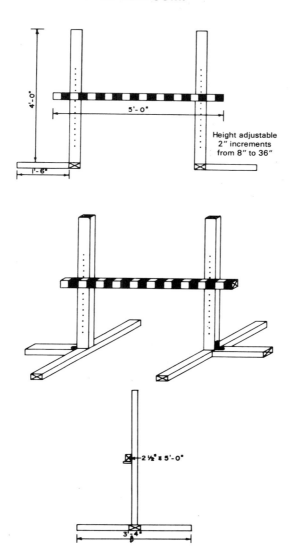

4'-0"

5'-0"

Height adjustable
2" increments
from 8" to 36"

1'-6"

2½" x 5'-0"

3'-4"

Section 16. **Disqualification and Ineligibility.** A dog that is blind or deaf or that has been changed in appearance by artificial means (except for such changes as are customarily approved for its breed) may not compete in any obedience trial or tracking test and must be disqualified. Blind means having useful vision in neither eye. Deaf means without useful hearing.

When a judge finds any of these conditions in any dog he is judging, he shall disqualify the dog marking his book "Disqualified" and stating the reason. He shall not obtain the opinion of the show veterinarian.

The judge must disqualify any dog that attempts to attack any person in the ring. He may excuse a dog that attacks another dog or that appears dangerous to other dogs in the ring. He shall mark the dog disqualified or excused and state the reason in his judge's book, and shall give the Superintendent or Show or Trial Secretary a brief report of the dog's actions which shall be submitted to AKC with the report of the show or trial.

When a dog has been disqualified under this section as being blind or deaf or having been changed in appearance by artificial means or for having attempted to attack a person in the ring, all awards made to the dog at the trial shall be cancelled by The American Kennel Club and the dog may not again compete unless and until, following application by the owner to The American Kennel Club, the owner has received official notification from The American Kennel Club that the dog's eligibility has been reinstated.

Spayed bitches, castrated dogs, monorchid or cryptorchid males, and dogs that have faults which would disqualify them under the standards for their breeds, may compete in obedience trials if otherwise eligible under these regulations.

A dog that is lame in the ring at any obedience trial or at a tracking test may not compete and shall not receive any score at the trial. It shall be the judge's responsibility to determine whether a dog is lame. He shall not obtain the opinion of the show veterinarian. If in the judge's opinion a dog in the ring is lame, he shall not score such dog, and shall promptly excuse it from the ring and mark his book "Excused—lame."

No dog shall be eligible to compete if it is taped or bandaged in any way or if it has anything attached to it for medical or corrective purposes. Such a dog must be immediately excused from the ring, and under no circumstance may it be returned later for judging after the tape, bandage or attachment has been removed.

With the exception of Maltese, Poodles, Shih Tzu and Yorkshire Terriers, which may be shown with the hair over the eyes tied back as they are normally shown in the breed ring, no dog shall be eligible to compete if it appears to have been dyed or colored in any way or if the coat shows evidence of chalk or powder, or if the dog has anything attached to it for protection or adornment. Such a dog may, at the judge's sole discretion, be judged at a later time if the offending condition has been corrected.

An obedience judge is not required to be familiar with the breed standards nor to scrutinize each dog as in dog show judging, but shall be alert for conditions which may require disqualification or exclusion under this section.

Section 17. **Disturbances.** Bitches in season are not permitted to compete. The judge of an obedience trial or tracking test must remove from competition any bitch in season, any dog which its handler cannot control, any handler who interferes willfully with another competitor or his dog, and any handler who abuses his dog in the ring, and may excuse from competition any dog which he considers unfit to compete, or any bitch which appears so attractive to males as to be a disturbing element. If a dog or handler is expelled or excused by a judge, the reason shall be stated in the judge's book or in a separate report.

Section 18. **Obedience Ribbons.** At licensed or member obedience trials the following colors shall be used for prize ribbons or rosettes in all regular classes for the ribbon or rosette for Highest Scoring Dog in the Regular Classes:

First Prize .... Blue
Second Prize .... Red
Third Prize .... Yellow
Fourth Prize .... White

144

Qualifying Prize .... Dark Green
Highest Scoring Dog
in the Regular Classes .... Blue and Gold
and the following colors shall be used for non-regular classes:
First Prize .... Rose
Second Prize .... Brown
Third Prize .... Light Green
Fourth Prize .... Gray
Each ribbon or rosette shall be at least two inches wide and approximately eight inches long, and shall bear on its face a facsimile of the seal of The American Kennel Club, the words "Obedience Trial," the name of the prize, the name of the trial-giving club, the date of the trial, and the name of the city or town where the trial is given.

Section 19. **Match Ribbons.** If ribbons are given at sanctioned obedience matches they shall be of the following colors and shall have the words "Obedience Match" printed on them, but may be of any design or size:
First Prize .... Rose
Second Prize .... Brown
Third Prize .... Light Green
Fourth Prize .... Gray
Qualifying Prize .... Green with Pink edges

Section 20. **Ribbons and Prizes.** Ribbons for the four official placings and all prizes offered for competition within a single regular or nonregular class at licensed or member trials or at sanctioned matches shall be awarded only to dogs that earn qualifying scores.

Prizes for which dogs in one class compete against dogs in one or more other classes at licensed or member trials or at sanctioned matches shall be awarded only to dogs that earn qualifying scores.

Prizes at a licensed or member obedience trial must be offered to be won outright, with the exception that a prize which requires three wins by the same owner, not necessarily with the same dog, for permanent possession, may be offered for the dog with the highest qualifying score in one of the regular classes, or the dog with the highest qualifying score in the regular classes, or the dog with the highest combined qualifying scores in the Open B and Utility classes.

Subject to the provisions of paragraphs 1 and 2 of this section, prizes may be offered for the highest scoring dogs of the Groups as defined in Chapter 2 of the Dog Show Rules, or for the highest scoring dogs of any breeds, but not for a breed variety. Show varieties are not recognized for obedience. In accordance with Chapter 2, all Poodles are in the Non-Sporting Group and all Manchester Terriers in the Terrier Group.

Prizes offered only to members of certain clubs or organizations will not be approved for publication in premium lists.

Section 21. **Highest Scoring Dog in the Regular Classes.** The dog receiving the highest qualifying score in the regular classes shall be awarded the ribbon and any prizes offered for this placement, after the announcement of final scores of the last regular class to be judged. The Superintendent or Show or Trial Secretary shall mark the catalog to identify the dog receiving this award.

In case of a tie between dogs receiving the highest qualifying score in two or more regular classes, the dogs shall be tested again by having them perform at the same time some part or parts of the Heel Free exercise. The judge for the run-off shall be designated by the Bench Show or Obedience Trial Committee from among the judges of the obedience trial. When the run-off has been completed, the judge shall record the results on a special sheet which shall identify the dogs taking part in the run-off by catalog number, class and breed. When the judge has marked and signed the sheet, it shall be turned over to the Superintendent or Show or Trial Secretary who shall mark the catalog accordingly and forward the sheet to The American Kennel Club as part of the records of the trial.

Section 22. **Risk.** The owner or agent entering a dog in an obedience trial does so at his own risk and agrees to abide by the rules of The American Kennel Club and the Obedience Regulations.

Section 23. **Decisions.** At the trial the decisions of the judge shall be final in all matters affecting the scoring and the working of the dogs and their handlers. The Obedience Trial Committee, or the Bench Show Committee, if the trial is held by a show-giving club, shall decide all other matters arising at the trial, including protests against dogs made under Chapter 20 of the Dog Show Rules, subject, however, to the rules and regulations of The American Kennel Club.

Section 24. **Dogs Must Compete.** Any dog entered and received at a licensed or member obedience trial must compete in all exercises of all classes in which it is entered unless disqualified, expelled, or excused by the judge or by the Bench Show or Obedience Trial Committee, or unless excused by the official veterinarian to protect the health of the dog or of other dogs at the trial. The excuse of the official veterinarian must be in writing and must be approved by the Superintendent or Show or Trial Secretary, and must be submitted to The American Kennel Club with the report of the trial. The judge must report to The American Kennel Club any dog that is not brought back for the Group exercises.

Section 25. **Judging Program.** Any club holding a licensed or member obedience trial must prepare, after the entries have closed, a program showing the time scheduled for the judging of each of the classes. A copy of this program shall be mailed to the owner of each entered dog and to each judge, and the program shall be printed in the catalog. This program shall be based on the judging of no more than 8 Novice entries, 7 Open entries, or 6 Utility entries, per hour during the time the show or trial will be open as published in the premium list, taking into consideration the starting hour for judging if published in the premium list, and the availability of rings. No judge shall be scheduled to exceed this rate of judging. In addition, one hour for rest or meals must be allowed if, under this formula, it will take more than five hours of actual judging to judge the dogs entered under him. No judge shall be assigned to judge for more than eight hours in one day under this formula, including any breed judging assignment if the obedience trial is held in conjunction with a dog show.

If any nonregular class is to be judged in the same ring as any regular class, or by the judge of any regular class, the nonregular class must be judged after the regular class.

Section 26. **Limitation of Entries.** If a club anticipates an entry in excess of its facilities for a licensed or member trial, it may limit entries in any or all regular classes, but nonregular classes will not be approved if the regular classes are limited. A club may limit entries in any or all regular classes to 64 in a Novice class, 56 in an Open class, or 48 in a Utility class.

Prominent announcement of such limits must appear on the title or cover page of the premium list for an obedience trial or immediately under the obedience heading in the premium list for a dog show, with a statement that entries in one or more specified classes or in the obedience trial will automatically close when a certain limit or limits have been reached, even though the official closing date for entries has not arrived.

Section 27. **Additional Judges, Reassignment, Split Classes.** If when the entries have closed, it is found that the entry under one or more judges exceeds the limit established in Section 25, the club shall immediately secure the approval of The American Kennel Club for the appointment of one or more additional judges, or for reassignment of its advertised judges, so that no judge will be required to exceed the limit.

If a judge with an excessive entry was advertised to judge more than one class, one or more of his classes shall be assigned to another judge. The class or classes selected for reassignment shall first be any nonregular classes for which he was advertised, and shall then be either the regular class or classes with the minimum number of entries, or those with the minimum scheduled time, which will bring the advertised judge's schedule within, and as close as possible to, the maximum limit. If a judge with an excessive entry was advertised to judge only one class, the Superinten-

146

dent, Show Secretary, or Obedience Trial Secretary, shall divide the entry as evenly as possible between the advertised judge and the other judge by drawing lots.

The club shall promptly mail to the owner of each entry affected, a notification of any change of judge. The owner shall be permitted to withdraw such entry at any time prior to the day of the show, and the entry fee shall then be refunded. If the entry in any one class is split in this manner, the advertised judge shall judge the run-off of any tie scores that may develop between the two divisions of the class, after each judge has first run off any ties resulting from his own judging.

Section 28. Split Classes in Premium List. A club may choose to announce two or more judges for any class in its premium list. In such case the entries shall be divided by lots as provided above. The identification slips and judging program shall be made up so that the owner of each dog will know the division, and the judge of the division, in which his dog is entered, but no owner shall be entitled to a refund of entry fee. In such case the premium list shall also specify the judge for the run-off of any tie scores which may develop between the dogs in the different divisions, after each judge has first run off any ties resulting from his own judging.

Section 29. Split Classes, Official Ribbons, Prizes. A club which holds a split class, whether the split is announced in the premium list or made after entries close, shall not award American Kennel Club official ribbons in either division. The four dogs with the highest qualifying scores in the class, regardless of the division or divisions in which such scores were made, shall be called back into the ring and awarded the four American Kennel Club official ribbons by one of the judges of the class. This judge shall be responsible for recording the entry numbers of the four placed dogs in one of the judges' books.

If a split class is announced in the premium list, duplicate placement prizes may be offered in each division. If prizes have been offered for placements in a class that must be split after entries close, duplicate prizes or prizes of equal value may be offered in the additional division of the class.

Section 30. Stewards. The judge is in sole charge of his ring until his assignment is completed. Stewards are provided to assist him, but they may act only on the judge's instructions. Stewards shall not give information or instructions to owners and handlers except as specifically instructed by the judge, and then only in such a manner that it is clear that the instructions are those of the judge.

Section 31. Ring Conditions. If the judging takes place indoors the ring should be rectangular and should be about 35' wide and 50' long for all obedience classes. In no case shall the ring for a Utility class be less than 35' by 50', and in no case shall the ring for a Novice or Open class be less than 30' by 40'. The floor shall have a surface or covering that provides firm footing for the largest dogs, and rubber or similar non-slip material must be laid for the take off and landing at all jumps unless the surface, in the judge's opinion, is such as not to require it. At an outdoor show or trial the rings shall be about 40' wide and 50' long. The ground shall be clean and level, and the grass, if any, shall be cut short. The Club and Superintendent are responsible for providing, for the Open classes, an appropriate place approved by the judge, for the handlers to go completely out of sight of their dogs. If inclement weather at an outdoor trial necessitates the judging of obedience under shelter, the requirements as to ring size may be waived.

Section 32. Obedience Rings at Dog Shows. At an outdoor dog show a separate ring or rings shall be provided for obedience, and a sign forbidding anyone to permit any dog to use the ring, except when being judged, shall be set up in each such ring by the Superintendent or Show Secretary. It shall be his duty as well as that of the Show Committee to enforce this regulation. At an indoor show where limited space does not permit the exclusive use of any ring for obedience, the same regulation will apply after the obedience rings have been set up. At a dog show the material used for enclosing the obedience rings shall be at least equal to the material used for enclosing the breed rings. The ring must be thoroughly cleaned before the obedience judging starts if it has previously been used for breed judging.

147

Section 33. **Judge's Report on Ring and Equipment.** The Superintendent and the officials of the club holding the obedience trial are responsible for providing rings and equipment which meet the requirements of these regulations. However, the judge must check the ring and equipment provided for his use before starting to judge, and must report to The American Kennel Club after the trial any undesirable ring conditions or deficiencies that have not been promptly corrected at his request.

CHAPTER 2

Regulations for Performance and Judging

Section 1. **Standardized Judging.** Standardized judging is of paramount importance. Judges are not permitted to inject their own variations into the exercises, but must see that each handler and dog executes the various exercises exactly as described in these regulations. A handler who is familiar with these regulations should be able to enter the ring under any judge without having to inquire how the particular judge wishes to have any exercise performed, and without being confronted with some unexpected requirement.

Section 2. **Standard of Perfection.** The judge must carry a mental picture of the theoretically perfect performance in each exercise and score each dog and handler against this visualized standard which shall combine the utmost in willingness, enjoyment and precision on the part of the dog, and naturalness, gentleness, and smoothness in handling. Lack of willingness or enjoyment on the part of the dog must be penalized, as must lack of precision in the dog's performance, roughness in handling, military precision or peremptory commands by the handler. There shall be no penalty of less than ½ point or multiple of ½ point.

Section 3. **Qualifying Performance.** A judge's certification in his judge's book of a qualifying score for any particular dog constitutes his certification to The American Kennel Club that the dog on this particular occasion has performed all of the required exercises at least in accordance with the minimum standards and that its performance on this occasion would justify the awarding of the obedience title associated with the particular class. A qualifying score must never be awarded to a dog whose performance has not met the minimum requirements, nor to a dog that shows fear or resentment, or that relieves itself at any time while in an indoor ring for judging, or that relieves itself while performing any exercise in an outdoor ring, nor to a dog whose handler disciplines or abuses it in the ring, or carries or offers food in the ring.
In deciding whether a faulty performance of a particular exercise by a particular dog warrants a qualifying score, the judge shall consider whether the awarding of an obedience title would be justified if all dogs in the class performed the exercise in a similar manner. The judge must not give a qualifying score for the exercise if he decides that it would be contrary to the best interests of the sport if all dogs in the class were to perform in the same way.

Section 4. **Judge's Directions.** The judge's orders and signals should be given to the handlers in a clear and understandable manner, but in such a way that the work of the dog is not disturbed. Before starting each exercise, the judge shall ask "Are you ready?" At the end of each exercise the judge shall say "Exercise finished." Each contestant must be worked and judged separately except for the Group exercises, and in running off a tie.

Section 5. **No Added Requirements.** No judge shall require any dog or handler to do anything, nor penalize a dog or handler for failing to do anything, that is not required by these regulations.

Section 6. **A and B Classes and Different Breeds.** The same methods and standards must be used for judging and scoring the A and B Classes, and in judging and scoring the work of dogs of different breeds.

148

Section 7. **Interference and Double Handling.** A judge who is aware of any assistance, interference, or attempts to control a dog from outside the ring, must act promptly to stop any such double handling or interference, and shall penalize the dog substantially or, if in the judge's opinion the circumstances warrant, shall give the dog a score of zero for the exercise during which the aid was received.

Section 8. **Rejudging.** If a dog has failed in a particular part of an exercise, it shall not ordinarily be rejudged nor given a second chance; but if in the judge's opinion the dog's performance was prejudiced by peculiar and unusual conditions, the judge may at his own discretion rejudge the dog on the entire exercise.

Section 9. **Ties.** In case of a tie any prize in a Novice or Open class, the dogs shall be tested again by having them perform at the same time all or some part of the Heel Free exercise. In the Utility class the dogs shall perform at the same time all or some part of the Signal exercise. The original scores shall not be changed.

Section 10. **Judge's Book and Score Sheets.** The judge must enter the scores and sub-total score of each dog in the official judge's book immediately after each dog has been judged on the individual exercises and before judging the next dog. Scores for the group exercises and total scores must be entered in the official judge's book immediately after each group of dogs has been judged. No score may be changed except to correct an arithmetical error or if a score has been entered in the wrong column. All final scores must be entered in the judge's book before prizes are awarded. No person other than the judge may make any entry in the judge's book. Judges may use separate score sheets for their own purposes, but shall not give out nor allow exhibitors to see such sheets, nor give out any other written scores, nor permit anyone else to distribute score sheets or cards prepared by the judge. Carbon copies of the sheets in the official judge's book shall be made available through the Superintendent or Show or Trial Secretary for examination by owners and handlers immediately after the prizes have been awarded in each class. If score cards are distributed by a club after the prizes are awarded they must contain no more information than is shown in the judge's book and must be marked "unofficial score."

Section 11. **Announcement of Scores.** The judge shall not disclose any score or partial score to contestants or spectators until he has completed the judging of the entire class or, in case of a split class, until he has completed the judging of his division; nor shall he permit anyone else to do so. After all the scores are recorded for the class, or for the division in case of a split class, the judge shall call for all available dogs that have won qualifying scores to be brought into the ring. Before awarding the prizes, the judge shall inform the spectators as to the maximum number of points for a perfect score, and shall then announce the score of each prize winner, and announce to the handler the score of each dog that has won a qualifying score.

Section 12. **Explanations and Errors.** The judge is not required to explain his scoring, and need not enter into any discussion with any contestant who appears to be dissatisfied. Any interested person who thinks that there may have been an arithmetical error or an error in identifying a dog may report the facts to one of the stewards or to the Superintendent or Show or Trial Secretary so that the matter may be checked.

Section 13. **Compliance with Regulations and Standards.** In accordance with the certification on the entry form, the handler of each dog and the person signing each entry form must be familiar with the Obedience Regulations applicable to the class in which the dog is entered.

Section 14. **Handicapped Handlers.** Judges may modify the specific requirements of these regulations for handlers to the extent necessary to permit physically handicapped handlers to compete, provided such handlers can move about the ring without physical assistance or guidance from another person, except for guidance from the judge or from the handler of a competing dog in the ring for the Group exercises.

149

Dogs handled by such handlers shall be required to perform all parts of all exercises as described in these regulations, and shall be penalized for failure to perform any part of an exercise.

Section 15. **Catalog Order.** Dogs should be judged in catalog order to the extent that it is practicable to do so without holding up the judging in any ring.

Judges are not required to wait for dogs for either the individual exercises or the group exercises. It is the responsibility of each handler to be ready with his dog at ringside when required, without being called. The judge's first consideration should be the convenience of those exhibitors who are at ringside with their dogs when scheduled, and who ask no favors.

A judge may agree, on request in advance of the scheduled starting time of the class, to judge a dog earlier or later than the time scheduled by catalog order. However, a judge should not hesitate to mark absent and to refuse to judge any dog and handler that are not at ringside ready to be judged in catalog order if no arrangement has been made in advance.

Section 16. **Use of Leash.** All dogs shall be kept on leash except when in the obedience ring or exercise ring. Dogs should be brought into the ring and taken out of the ring on leash. Dogs may be kept on leash in the ring when brought in to receive awards, and when waiting in the ring before and after the Group exercises. The leash shall be left on the judge's table or other designated place, between the individual exercises, and during all exercises except the Heel on Leash and Group exercises. The leash may be of fabric or leather and, in the Novice classes, need be only of sufficient length to provide adequate slack in the Heel on Leash exercise.

Section 17. **Collars.** Dogs in the obedience ring must wear well-fitting plain buckle or slip collars. Slip collars of an appropriate single length of leather, fabric or chain with two rings, one on each end are acceptable. Fancy collars, or special training collars, or collars that are either too tight or so large that they hang down unreasonably in front of the dogs, are not permitted. There shall not be anything hanging from the collars.

Section 18. **Heel Position.** The heel position as used in these regulations, whether the dog is sitting, standing, or moving at heel, means that the dog shall be straight in line with the direction in which the handler is facing, at the handler's left side, and as close as practicable to the handler's left leg without crowding, permitting the handler freedom of motion at all times. The area from the dog's head to shoulder shall be in line with the handler's left hip.

Section 19. **Hands.** In all exercises in which the dog is required to come to or return to the handler and sit in front, the handler's arms and hands shall hang naturally at his sides while the dog is coming in and until the dog has sat in front. A substantial deduction shall be made if a handler's arms and hands are not hanging naturally at his sides.

Section 20. **Commands and Signals.** Whenever a command or signal is mentioned in these regulations, a single command or signal only may be given by the handler, and any extra commands or signals must be penalized; except that whenever the regulations specify "command and/or signal" the handler may give either one or the other or both command and signal simultaneously. When a signal is permitted and given, it must be a single gesture with one arm and hand only, and the arm must immediately be returned to a natural position. Delay in following a judge's order to give a command or signal must be penalized, unless the delay is directed by the judge because of some distraction or interference.

The signal for downing a dog may be given either with the arm raised or with a down swing of the arm, but any pause in holding the arm upright followed by a down swing of the arm will be considered an additional signal.

Signaling correction to a dog is forbidden and must be penalized. Signals must be inaudible and the handler must not touch the dog. Any unusual noise or motion may be considered to be a signal. Movements of the body that aid the dog shall be considered additional signals except that a handler may bend as far as necessary to bring his hand on a level with the dog's eyes in giving a signal to a dog in the heel position, and that in the Directed Retrieve exercise the body and knees may be bent to the extent necessary to give the direction to the dog. Whistling or the use of a whistle is prohibited.

The dog's name may be used once immediately before any verbal command or before a verbal command and signal when these regulations permit command and/or signal. The name shall not be used with any signal not given simultaneously with a verbal command. The dog's name, when given immediately before a verbal command, shall not be considered as an additional command, but a dog that responds to its name without waiting for the verbal command shall be scored as having anticipated the command. The dog should never anticipate the handler's directions, but must wait for the appropriate commands and/or signals. Moving forward at heel without any command or signal other than the natural movement of the handler's left leg, shall not be considered as anticipation.

Loud commands by handlers to their dogs create a poor impression of obedience and should be avoided. Shouting is not necessary even in a noisy place if the dog is properly trained to respond to a normal tone of voice. Commands which in the judge's opinion are excessively loud will be penalized.

Section 21. **Additional Commands or Signals.** If a handler gives an additional command or signal not permitted by these regulations, either when no command or signal is permitted, or simultaneously with or following a permitted command or signal, or if he uses the dog's name with a permitted signal but without a permitted command, the dog shall be scored as though it had failed completely to perform that particular part of the exercise.

Section 22. **Praise.** Praise and petting are allowed between and after exercises, but points must be deducted from the total score for a dog that is not under reasonable control while being praised. A handler shall not carry or offer food in the ring. There shall be a substantial penalty for any dog that is picked up or carried at any time in the obedience ring.

Section 23. **Handling between Exercises.** In the Novice classes the dog may be guided gently by the collar between exercises and to get it into proper position for an exercise. No other physical guidance, such as placing the dog in position with the hands or straightening the dog with the knees or feet, is permitted and shall be substantially penalized even if occurring before or between the exercises.

In the Open and Utility classes there shall be a substantial penalty for any dog that is physically guided at any time or that is not readily controllable.

Posing for examination and holding for measurement are permitted. Imperfections in heeling between exercises will not be judged. Minor penalties shall be imposed for a dog that does not respond promptly to its handler's commands or signals before or between exercises in the Open and Utility classes.

Section 24. **Orders and Minimum Penalties.** The orders for the exercises and the standards for judging are set forth in the following chapters. The lists of faults are not intended to be complete but minimum penalties are specified for most of the more common and serious faults. There is no maximum limit on penalties. A dog which makes none of the errors listed may still fail to qualify or may be scored zero for other reasons.

Section 25. **Misbehavior.** Any disciplining by the handler in the ring, any display of fear or nervousness by the dog, or any uncontrolled behavior of the dog such as snapping, barking, relieving itself while in the ring for judging, or running away from its handler, whether it occurs during an exercise, between exercises, or before or after judging, must be penalized according to the seriousness of the misbehavior, and the judge may expel or excuse the dog from further competition in the class. If such behavior occurs during an exercise, the penalty must first be applied to the score for that exercise. Should the penalty be greater than the value of the exercise during which it is incurred, the additional points shall be deducted from the total score under Misbehavior. If such behavior occurs before or after the judging or between exercises, the entire penalty shall be deducted from the total score.

The judge must disqualify any dog that attempts to attack any person in the ring. He may excuse a dog that attacks another dog or that appears dangerous to other dogs in the ring.

151

Section 26. **Training on the Grounds.** There shall be no drilling nor intensive or abusive training of dogs on the grounds or premises at a licensed or member obedience trial or at a sanctioned match. No practice rings or areas shall be permitted at such events. All dogs shall be kept on leash except when in the obedience ring or exercise ring. Special training collars shall not be used on the grounds or premises at an obedience trial or match. These requirements shall not be interpreted as preventing a handler from moving normally about the grounds or premises with his dog at heel on leash, nor from giving such signals or such commands in a normal tone, as are necessary and usual in everyday life in heeling a dog or making it stay, but physical or verbal disciplining of dogs shall not be permitted except to a reasonable extent in the case of an attack on a person or another dog. The Superintendent, or Show or Trial Secretary, and the members of the Bench Show or Obedience Trial Committee, shall be responsible for compliance with this section, and shall investigate any reports of infractions.

Section 27. **Training and Disciplining in the Ring.** The judge shall not permit any handler to train his dog nor to practice any exercise in the ring either before or after he is judged, and shall deduct points from the total score of any dog whose handler does this. A dog whose handler disciplines it in the ring must not receive a qualifying score. The penalty shall be deducted from the points available for the exercise during which the disciplining may occur, and additional points may be deducted from the total score if necessary. If the disciplining does not occur during an exercise the penalty shall be deducted from the total score. Any abuse of a dog in the ring must be immediately reported by the judge to the Bench Show or Obedience Trial Committee for action under Chapter 2, Section 29.

Section 28. **Abuse of Dogs.** The Bench Show or Obedience Trial Committee shall investigate any reports of abuse of dogs or severe disciplining of dogs on the grounds or premises of a show, trial or match. Any person who, at a licensed or member obedience trial, conducts himself in such manner or in any other manner prejudicial to the best interests of the sport, or who fails to comply with the requirements of Chapter 2, Section 26, shall be dealt with promptly, during the trial if possible, after the offender has been notified of the specific charges against him, and has been given an opportunity to be heard in his own defense in accordance with Chapter 2, Section 29.

Any abuse of a dog in the ring must be immediately reported by the judge to the Bench Show or Obedience Trial Committee for action under Chapter 2, Section 29.

Article XII Section 2 of the Constitution and By-Laws of The American Kennel Club Provides:

Section 29. **Discipline.** The Bench Show, Obedience Trial or Field Trial Committee of a club or association shall have the right to suspend any person from the privileges of The American Kennel Club for conduct prejudicial to the best interests of pure-bred dogs, dog shows, obedience trials, field trials or The American Kennel Club, alleged to have occurred in connection with or during the progress of its show, obedience trial or field trial, after the alleged offender has been given an opportunity to be heard.

Notice in writing must be sent promptly by registered mail by the Bench Show, Obedience Trial or Field Trial Committee to the person suspended and a duplicate notice giving the name and address of the person suspended and full details as to the reasons for the suspensvn must be forwarded to The American Kennel Club within seven days.

An appeal may be taken from a decision of a Bench Show, Obedience Trial or Field Trial Committee. Notice in writing claiming such appeal together with a deposit of five ($5.00) dollars must be sent to The American Kennel Club within thirty days after the date of suspension. The Board of Directors may itself hear said appeal or may refer it to a committee of the Board, or to a Trial Board to be heard. The deposit shall become the property of The American Kennel Club if the decision is confirmed, or shall be returned to the appellant if the decision is not confirmed.

(See Guide for Bench Show and Obedience Trial Committees in Dealing with Misconduct at Dog Shows and Obedience Trials for proper procedure at licensed or member obedience trials.)

(The Committee at a Sanctioned event does not have this power of suspension, but must investigate any allegation of such conduct and forward a complete and detailed report of any such incident to The American Kennel Club.)

CHAPTER 3
NOVICE

Section 1. **Novice A Class.** The Novice A class shall be for dogs not less than six months of age that have not won the title C.D. A dog that is owned or co-owned by a person who has previously handled or regularly trained a dog that has won a C.D. title may not be entered in the Novice A class, nor may a dog be handled in this class by such person.

Each dog in this class must have a different handler who shall be its owner or co-owner or a member of the immediate family of the owner or co-owner, provided that such member has not previously handled or regularly trained a C.D. dog. The same person must handle the same dog in all exercises. No person may handle more than one dog in the Novice A class.

Section 2. **Novice B Class.** The Novice B class shall be for dogs not less than six months of age that have not won the title C.D. Dogs in this class may be handled by the owner or any other person. A person may handle more than one dog in this class, but each dog must have a separate handler for the Long Sit and Long Down exercises when judged in the same group. No dog may be entered in both Novice A and Novice B classes at any one trial.

Section 3. **Novice Exercises and Scores.** The exercises and maximum scores in the Novice classes are:

1. Heel on Leash .... 40 points
2. Stand for Examination .... 30 points
3. Heel Free .... 40 points
4. Recall .... 30 points
5. Long Sit .... 30 points
6. Long Down .... 30 points
   Maximum Total Score .... 200 points

Section 4. **C.D. Title.** The American Kennel Club will issue a Companion Dog certificate for each registered dog, and will permit the use of the letters "C.D." after the name of each dog that has been certified by three different judges to have received qualifying scores in Novice classes at three licensed or member obedience trials, provided the sum total of dogs that actually competed in the regular Novice classes at each trial is not less than six.

Section 5. **Heel on Leash & Figure Eight.** The principal feature of this exercise is the ability of the dog and handler to work as a team.

Orders for the exercise are "Forward," "Halt," "Right turn," "Left turn," "About turn," "Slow," "Normal" and "Fast." "Fast" signifies that the handler must run, handler and dog moving forward at noticeably accelerated speed. In executing the About turn, the handler will always do a Right About turn.

The orders may be given in any sequence and may be repeated as necessary, but the judge shall attempt to standardize the heeling pattern for all dogs in any class.

The leash may be held in either hand or in both hands, provided the hands are in a natural position. However, any tightening or jerking of the leash or any act, signal or command which in the judge's opinion gives the dog assistance shall be penalized.

The handler shall enter the ring with his dog on a loose leash and stand with the dog sitting in the Heel Position. The judge shall ask if the handler is ready before giving the order, "Forward." The handler may give a command or signal to Heel, and shall walk briskly and in a natural manner with his dog on a loose leash. The dog shall walk close to the left side of the handler without swinging wide, lagging, forging or crowding. Whether heeling or sitting, the dog must not interfere with the handler's freedom of motion at any time. At each order to Halt, the handler will stop and his dog shall sit straight and promptly in the Heel Position without command or signal, and shall not move until the handler again moves forward on order from the judge. It is permissible after each Halt, before moving again, for the handler to give a command or signal to Heel. The judge shall say, "Exercise finished" after this portion of the exercise.

Before starting the Figure Eight the judge shall ask if the handler is ready. Figure Eight signifies that on specific orders from the judge to Forward and Halt, the handler and dog, from a starting position midway between two stewards and facing the judge, shall walk briskly twice completely around and between the two stewards, who shall stand 8 feet apart. The Figure Eight in the Novice classes shall be done on leash. The handler may choose to go in either direction. There shall be no About turn or Fast or Slow in the Figure Eight, but the judge must order at least one Halt during and another Halt at the end of this portion of the exercise.

Section 6. **Heel on Leash & Figure Eight Scoring.** If a dog is unmanageable, or if its handler constantly controls its performance by tugging on the leash or adapts pace to that of the dog, the dog must be scored zero.

Substantial deductions shall be made for additional commands or signals to Heel and for failure of dog or handler to change pace noticeably for Slow and Fast.

Substantial or Minor deductions shall be made for such things as lagging, heeling wide, poor sits, handler failing to walk at a brisk pace, occasional guidance with leash and other imperfections in heeling.

In scoring this exercise the judge shall accompany the handler at a discreet distance so that he can observe any signals or commands given by the handler to the dog. The judge must do so without interfering with either dog or handler.

Section 7. **Stand for Examination.** The principal features of this exercise are that the dog stand in position before and during the examination, and that the dog display neither shyness nor resentment.

Orders are "Stand your dog and leave when you are ready," "Back to your dog" and "Exercise finished." There will be no further command from the judge to the handler to leave the dog.

The handler shall take his dog on leash to a place indicated by the judge, where the handler shall remove the leash and give it to a steward who shall place it on the judge's table or other designated place.

On judge's order the handler will stand and/or pose his dog off leash by the method of his choice, taking any reasonable time if he chooses to pose the dog as in the show ring. When he is ready, the handler will give his command and/or signal to the dog to Stay, walk forward about six feet in front of the dog, turn around and stand facing the dog.

The judge shall approach the dog from the front, and shall touch only the dog's head, body and hindquarters, using the fingers and palm of one hand only. He shall then order, "Back to your dog," whereupon the handler shall walk around behind his dog and return to the Heel Position. The dog must remain standing until after the judge has said, "Exercise finished."

Section 8. **Stand for Examination, Scoring.** The scoring of this exercise will not start until the handler has given the command and/or signal to Stay, except for such things as rough treatment of the dog by its handler or active resistance by the dog to its handler's attempts to make it stand. Either of these shall be penalized substantially.

A dog that displays any shyness or resentment or growls or snaps at any time shall be scored zero, as shall a dog that sits before or during the examination or a dog that moves away before or during the examination from the place where it was left.

Minor or substantial deductions, depending on the circumstance, shall be made for a dog that moves its feet at any time or sits or moves away after the examination has been completed.

Section 9. **Heel Free, Performance and Scoring.** This exercise shall be executed in the same manner as Heel on Leash & Figure Eight except that the dog shall be off leash and that there shall be no Figure Eight. Orders and scoring shall also be the same.

Section 10. **Recall.** The principal features of this exercise are that the dog stay where left until

154

called by its handler, and that the dog respond promptly to the handler's command or signal to Come.

Orders are "Leave your dog," "Call your dog" and "Finish."

On order from the judge, the handler may give command and/or signal to the dog to Stay in the sit position while the handler walks forward about 35 feet to the other end of the ring, where he shall turn and stand in a natural manner facing his dog. On judge's order or signal, the handler will give command or signal for the dog to Come. The dog must come straight in at a brisk pace and sit straight, centered immediately in front of the handler's feet, close enough that the handler could readily touch its head without moving either foot or having to stretch forward. The dog must not touch the handler or sit between his feet.

On judge's order the handler will give command or signal to Finish and the dog must go smartly to the Heel Position and sit. The manner in which the dog finishes shall be optional with the handler provided that it is prompt and that the dog sit straight at heel.

Section 11. **Recall, Scoring.** A dog must receive a score of zero for the following: not staying without additional command or signal, failure to come on the first command or signal, moving from the place where left before being called or signalled, not sitting close enough in front that the handler could readily touch its head without moving either foot or stretching forward.

Substantial deductions shall be made for a slow response to the Come, varying with the extent of the slowness; for extra command or signal to Stay if given before the handler leaves the dog; for the dog's standing or lying down instead of waiting in the sit position; for extra command or signal to Finish and for failure to Sit or Finish.

Minor deductions shall be made for slow or poor Sits or Finishes, for touching the handler on coming in or while finishing, and for sitting between the handler's feet.

Section 12. **Group Exercises.** The principal feature of these exercises is that the dog remain in the sitting or down position, whichever is required by the particular exercise.

Orders are "Sit your dogs" or "Down your dogs," "Leave your dogs" and "Back to your dogs."

All the competing dogs in the class take these exercises together, except that if there are 12 or more dogs they shall, at the judge's option, be judged in groups of not less than 6 nor more than 15 dogs. When the same judge does both Novice A and Novice B, the two classes may be combined provided that there are not more than 15 dogs competing in combined classes. The dogs that are in the ring shall be lined up in catalog order along one of the four sides of the ring. Handlers' armbands, weighted with leashes or other articles if necessary, shall be placed behind the dogs.

For the Long Sit the handlers shall, on order from the judge, command and/or signal their dogs to Sit if they are not already sitting. On further order from the judge to leave their dogs, the handlers shall give a command and/or signal to Stay and immediately leave their dogs. The handlers will go to the opposite side of the ring, turn and stand facing their respective dogs.

If a dog gets up and starts to roam or follows its handler, or if a dog moves so as to interfere with another dog, the judge shall promptly instruct the handler or one of the stewards to take the dog out of the ring or to keep it away from the other dogs.

After one minute from the time he has ordered the handlers to leave their dogs, the judge will give the order to return, whereupon the handlers must promptly go back to their dogs, each walking around and in back of his own dog to the Heel Position. The dogs must not move from the sitting position until after the judge has said, "Exercise finished." The judge shall not give the order "Exercise finished" until the handlers have returned to the Heel Position.

Before starting the Long Down the judge shall ask if the handlers are ready. The Long Down is done in the same manner as the Long Sit except that instead of sitting their dogs the handlers shall, on order from the judge, down their dogs without touching either the dogs or their collars, and except further that the judge will order the handlers to return after three minutes. The dogs must not move from the down position until after the judge has said, "Exercise finished."

The dogs shall not be required to sit at the end of the Down exercise.

Section 13. **Group Exercises, Scoring.** During these exercises the judge shall stand in such position that all of the dogs are in his line of vision, and where he can see all the handlers in the ring without having to turn around.

Scoring of the exercises will not start until after the judge has ordered the handlers to leave their dogs, except for such things as rough treatment of a dog by its handler or active resistance by a dog to its handler's attempts to make it Sit or lie Down. These shall be penalized substantially; in extreme cases the dog may be excused.

A score of zero is required for the following: the dog's moving at any time during either exercise a substantial distance away from the place where it was left, or going over to any other dog, or staying on the spot where it was left but not remaining in whichever position is required by the particular exercise until the handler has returned to the Heel Position, or repeatedly barking or whining.

A substantial deduction shall be made for a dog that moves even a minor distance away from the place where it was left or that barks or whines only once or twice. Depending on the circumstance, a substantial or minor deduction shall be made for touching the dog or its collar in getting the dog into the Down position.

There shall be a minor deduction if a dog changes position after the handler has returned to the Heel Position but before the judge has said, "Exercise finished." The judge shall not give the order "Exercise finished" until the handlers have returned to the Heel Position.

CHAPTER 4
OPEN

Section 1. **Open A Class.** The Open A class shall be for dogs that have won the C.D. title but have not won the title C.D.X. Obedience judges and licensed handlers may not enter or handle dogs in this class. Each dog must be handled by its owner or by a member of his immediate family. Owners may enter more than one dog in this class but the same person who handled each dog in the first five exercises must handle the same dog in the Long Sit and Long Down exercises, except that if a person has handled more than one dog in the first five exercises he must have an additional handler, who must be the owner or a member of his immediate family, for each additional dog, when more than one dog that he has handled in the first five exercises is judged in the same group for the Long Sit and Long Down.

Section 2. **Open B Class.** The Open B class will be for dogs that have won the title C.D. or C.D.X. A dog may continue to compete in this class after it has won the title U.D. Dogs in this class may be handled by the owner or any other person. Owners may enter more than one dog in this class but the same person who handled each dog in the first five exercises must handle each dog in the Long Sit and Long Down exercises, except that if a person has handled more than one dog in the first five exercises he must have an additional handler for each additional dog, when more than one dog that he has handled in the first five exercises is judged in the same group for the Long Sit and Long Down. No dog may be entered in both Open A and Open B classes at any one trial.

Section 3. **Open Exercises and Scores.** The exercises and maximum scores in the Open classes are:

1. Heel Free .... 40 points
2. Drop on Recall .... 30 points
3. Retrieve on Flat .... 20 points
4. Retrieve over High Jump .... 30 points
5. Broad Jump .... 20 points
6. Long Sit .... 30 points
7. Long Down .... 30 points
   Maximum Total Score .... 200 points

156

Section 4. **C.D.X. Title.** The American Kennel Club will issue a Companion Dog Excellent certificate for each registered dog, and will permit the use of the letters "C.D.X." after the name of each dog that has been certified by three different judges of obedience trials to have received qualifying scores in Open classes at three licensed or member obedience trials, provided the sum total of dogs that actually competed in the regular Open classes at each trial is not less than six.

Section 5. **Heel Free, Performance and Scoring.** This exercise shall be executed in the same manner as the Novice Heel on Leash and Figure Eight exercise, except that the dog is off leash. Orders and scoring are the same as in Heel on Leash and Figure Eight.

Section 6. **Drop on Recall.** The principal features of this exercise, in addition to those listed under the Novice Recall, are the dog's prompt response to the handler's command or signal to Drop, and the dog's remaining in the Down position until again called or signalled to Come. The dog will be judged on the promptness of its response to command or signal and not on its proximity to a designated point.

Orders for the exercise are "Leave your dog," "Call your dog," an order or signal to Drop the dog, another "Call your dog" and "Finish." The judge may designate in advance a point at which, as the dog is coming in, the handler shall give his command or signal to the dog to Drop. The judge's signal or designated point must be clear to the handler but not obvious or distracting to the dog.

On order from the judge, the handler may give command and/or signal for the dog to Stay in the sit position while the handler walks forward about 35 feet to the other end of the ring, where he shall turn and stand in a natural manner facing his dog. On judge's order or signal, the handler shall give command or signal to Come and the dog must start straight in at a brisk pace. On judge's order or signal, or at a point designated in advance by the judge, the handler shall give command or signal to Drop, and the dog must immediately drop completely to the down position, where he must remain until, on judge's order or signal, the handler again gives command or signal to Come. The dog must come straight in at a brisk pace and sit straight, centered immediately in front of the handler's feet, close enough that the handler could readily touch the dog's head without moving either foot or having to stretch forward. The dog must not touch the handler nor sit between his feet.

The Finish shall be executed as in the Novice Recall.

Section 7. **Drop on Recall, Scoring.** All applicable penalties listed under the Novice Recall as requiring a score of zero shall apply. In addition, a zero score is required for a dog that does not drop completely to the down position on a single command or signal, and for a dog that drops but does not remain down until called or signalled.

Substantial deductions, varying with the extent, shall be made for delayed or slow response to the handler's command or signal to Drop, for slow response to either of the Comes, for extra command or signal to Stay if given before the handler leaves the dog, for the dog's standing or lying down instead of waiting where left in a sit position, for extra command or signal to Finish and for failure to finish.

Minor deductions shall be made for slow or poor sits or finishes, for touching the handler on coming in or while finishing, or for sitting between the handler's feet.

Section 8. **Retrieve on the Flat.** The principal feature of this exercise is that the dog retrieve promptly.

Orders are "Throw it," "Send your dog," "Take it" and "Finish."

The handler shall stand with his dog sitting in the Heel Position in a place designated by the judge. On order, "Throw it," the handler shall give command and/or signal to Stay, which signal may not be given with the hand that is holding the dumbbell, and throw the dumbbell. On order to send his dog, the handler shall give command or signal to retrieve. The retrieve shall be executed at a fast trot or gallop, the dog going directly to the dumbbell and retrieving it without unnecessary mouthing or playing with the dumbbell. The dog must sit straight to deliver, centered immediately in front of the handler's feet, close enough that the handler can readily take the dumbbell without moving either foot or having to stretch forward. The dog must not touch the handler nor sit between his feet. On order from the judge to take it, the handler shall give command or signal and take the dumbbell.

The finish shall be executed as in the Novice Recall.

The dumbbell, which must be approved by the judge, shall be made of one or more solid pieces of one of the heavy hardwoods, which shall not be hollowed out. It may be unfinished, or coated with a clear finish, or painted white. It shall have no decorations or attachments but may bear an inconspicuous mark for identification. The size of the dumbbell shall be proportionate to the size of the dog. The judge shall require the dumbbell to be thrown again before the dog is sent if, in his opinion, it is thrown too short a distance, or too far to one side, or too close to the ringside.

Section 9. **Retrieve on the Flat, Scoring.** A dog that fails to go out on the first command or signal, or goes to retrieve before the command or signal is given, or fails to retrieve, or does not return with the dumbbell sufficiently close that the handler can easily take the dumbbell as described above, must be scored zero.

Substantial deductions, depending on the extent, shall be made for slowness in going out or returning or in picking up the dumbbell, for not going directly to the dumbbell, for mouthing or playing with or dropping the dumbbell, for reluctance or refusal to release the dumbbell to the handler, for extra command or signal to finish and for failure to sit or finish.

Substantial or minor deductions shall be made for slow or poor sits or finishes, for touching the handler on coming in or while finishing, or for sitting between the handler's feet.

Section 10. **Retrieve over High Jump.** The principal features of this exercise are that the dog go out over the jump, pick up the dumbbell and promptly return with it over the jump.

Orders are "Throw it," "Send your dog," "Take it" and "Finish."

This exercise shall be executed in the same manner as the Retrieve on the Flat, except that the dog must clear the High Jump both going and coming. The handler must stand at least eight feet, or any reasonable distance beyond 8 feet, from the jump but must remain in the same spot throughout the exercise.

The jump shall be as nearly as possible one and one-half times the height of the dog at the withers, as determined by the judge, with a minimum height of 8 inches and a maximum height of 36 inches. This applies to all breeds with the following exceptions:

The jump shall be once the height of the dog at the withers or 36 inches, whichever is less, for the following breeds—

Bloodhounds	Mastiffs
Bullmastiffs	Newfoundlands
Great Danes	St. Bernards
Great Pyrenees	

The jump shall be once the height of the dog at the withers or 8 inches, whichever is greater, for the following breeds—

Spaniels (Clumber)	Norwich Terriers
Spaniels (Sussex)	Scottish Terriers
Basset Hounds	Sealyham Terriers
Dachshunds	Skye Terriers
Welsh Corgis (Cardigan)	West Highland White Terriers
Welsh Corgis (Pembroke)	Maltese
Australian Terriers	Pekingese
Cairn Terriers	Bulldogs
Dandie Dinmont Terriers	French Bulldogs

The jumps may be preset by the stewards based on the handler's advice as to the dog's height. The judge must make certain that the jump is set at the required height for each dog. He shall verify in the ring with an ordinary folding rule or steel tape to the nearest one-half inch, the height at the withers of each dog that jumps less than 36 inches. He shall not base his decision as to the height of the jump on the handler's advice.

The side posts of the High Jump shall be 4 feet high and the jump shall be 5 feet wide and shall be so constructed as to provide adjustment for each 2 inches from 8 inches to 36 inches. It is suggested that the jump have a bottom board 8 inches wide including the space from the bottom of the board to the ground or floor, together with three other 8 inch boards, one 4 inch board, and one 2 inch board. A 6 inch board may also be provided. The jump shall be painted a flat white. The width in inches, and nothing else, shall be painted on each side of each board in black 2 inch figures, the figure on the bottom board representing the distance from the ground or floor to the top of the board.

Section 11. **Retrieve over High Jump, Scoring.** Scoring of this exercise shall be as in Retrieve on the Flat. In addition, a dog that fails, either going or returning, to go over the jump, or that climbs or uses the jump for aid in going over, must be scored zero. Touching the jump in going over is added to the substantial and minor penalties listed under Retrieve on the Flat.

Section 12. **Broad Jump.** The principal features of this exercise are that the dog stay sitting until directed to jump and that the dog clear the jump on a single command or signal.

Orders are "Leave your dog," "Send your dog" and "Finish."

The handler will stand with his dog sitting in the Heel Position in front of and at least 8 feet from the jump. On order from the judge to "Leave your dog," the handler will give his dog the command and/or signal to Stay and go to a position facing the right side of the jump, with his toes about 2 feet from the jump, and anywhere between the lowest edge of the first hurdle and the highest edge of the last hurdle.

On order from the judge the handler shall give the command or signal to jump and the dog shall clear the entire distance of the Broad Jump without touching and, without further command or signal, return to a sitting position immediately in front of the handler as in the Recall. The handler shall change his position by executing a right angle turn while the dog is in mid-air, but shall remain in the same spot. The dog must sit and finish as in the Novice Recall.

The Broad Jump shall consist of four hurdles, built to telescope for convenience, made of boards about 8 inches wide, the largest measuring about 5 feet in length and 6 inches high at the highest point, all painted a flat white. When set up they shall be arranged in order of size and shall be evenly spaced so as to cover a distance equal to twice the height of the High Jump as set for the particular dog, with the low side of each hurdle and the lowest hurdle nearest the dog. The four hurdles shall be used for a jump of 52″ to 72″, three for a jump of 32″ to 48″, and two for a jump of 16″ to 28″. The highest hurdles shall be removed first. It is the judge's responsibility to see that the distance jumped is that required by these Regulations for the particular dog.

Section 13. **Broad Jump, Scoring.** A dog that fails to stay until directed to jump, or refuses the jump on the first command or signal, or walks over any part of the jump, or fails to clear the full distance, with its forelegs, must be scored zero. Minor or substantial deductions, depending on the specific circumstances in each case, shall be made for a dog that touches the jump in going over or that does not return directly to the handler. All other applicable penalties listed under the Recall shall apply.

Section 14. **Open Group Exercises, Performance and Scoring.** During Long Sit and the Long Down exercises the judge shall stand in such a position that all of the dogs are in his line of vision, and where he can see all the handlers in the ring, or leaving and returning to the ring, without having to turn around.

These exercises in the Open classes are performed in the same manner as in the Novice classes except that after leaving their dogs the handlers must cross to the opposite side of the ring, and then leave the ring in single file as directed by the judge and go to a place designated by the judge, completely out of sight of their dogs, where they must remain until called by the judge after the expiration of the time limit of three minutes in the Long Sit and five minutes in the Long Down, from the time the judge gave the order to "Leave your dogs." On order from the judge the handlers shall return to the ring in single file in reverse order, lining up facing their dogs at the opposite side of the ring, and returning to their dogs on order from the judge.

BIBLIOGRAPHY

ALL OWNERS of pure-bred dogs will benefit themselves and their dogs by enriching their knowledge of breeds and of canine care, training, breeding, psychology and other important aspects of dog management. The following list of books covers further reading recommended by judges, veterinarians, breeders, trainers and other authorities. Books may be obtained at the finer book stores and pet shops, or through Howell Book House Inc., publishers, New York.

Breed Books

AFGHAN HOUND, Complete	Miller & Gilbert
AIREDALE, New Complete	Edwards
ALASKAN MALAMUTE, Complete	Riddle & Seeley
BASSET HOUND, Complete	Braun
BEAGLE, Complete	Noted Authorities
BLOODHOUND, Complete	Brey & Reed
BOXER, Complete	Denlinger
BRITTANY SPANIEL, Complete	Riddle
BULLDOG, New Complete	Hanes
BULL TERRIER, New Complete	Eberhard
CAIRN TERRIER, Complete	Marvin
CHIHUAHUA, Complete	Noted Authorities
COCKER SPANIEL, New	Kraeuchi
COLLIE, Complete	Official Publication of the
Collie Club of America	
DACHSHUND, The New	Meistrell
DOBERMAN PINSCHER, New	Walker
ENGLISH SETTER, New Complete	Tuck & Howell
ENGLISH SPRINGER SPANIEL, New	
Goodall & Gasow	
FOX TERRIER, New Complete	Silvernail
GERMAN SHEPHERD DOG, Complete	Bennett
GERMAN SHORTHAIRED POINTER, New	Maxwell
GOLDEN RETRIEVER, Complete	Fischer
GREAT DANE, New Complete	Noted Authorities
GREAT PYRENEES, Complete	Strang & Giffin
IRISH SETTER, New	Thompson
IRISH WOLFHOUND, Complete	Starbuck
KEESHOND, Complete	Peterson
LABRADOR RETRIEVER, Complete	Warwick
LHASA APSO, Complete	Herbel
MINIATURE SCHNAUZER, Complete	Eskrigge
NEWFOUNDLAND, New Complete	Chern
NORWEGIAN ELKHOUND, New Complete	Wallo
OLD ENGLISH SHEEPDOG, Complete	Mandeville
PEKINGESE, Quigley Book of	Quigley
PEMBROKE WELSH CORGI, Complete	
Sargent & Harper	
POMERANIAN, New Complete	Ricketts
POODLE, New Complete	Hopkins & Irick
POODLE CLIPPING AND GROOMING BOOK,	
Complete	Kalstone
PUG, Complete	Trullinger
PULI, Complete	Owen
ST. BERNARD, New Complete	
Noted Authorities, rev. Raulston	
SAMOYED, Complete	Ward
SCHIPPERKE, Official Book of	Root, Martin, Kent
SCOTTISH TERRIER, Complete	Marvin
SHETLAND SHEEPDOG, New	Riddle
SHIH TZU, The (English)	Dadds
SIBERIAN HUSKY, Complete	Demidoff
TERRIERS, The Book of All	Marvin
TOY DOGS, Kalstone Guide to Grooming All	
Kalstone	
TOY DOGS, All About	Ricketts
WEST HIGHLAND WHITE TERRIER,	
Complete	Marvin
WHIPPET, Complete	Pegram
YORKSHIRE TERRIER, Complete	
Gordon & Bennett	

Care and Training

DOG OBEDIENCE, Complete Book of	Saunders
NOVICE, OPEN AND UTILITY COURSES	
Saunders	
DOG CARE AND TRAINING, Howell	
Book of	Howell, Denlinger, Merrick
DOG CARE AND TRAINING FOR BOYS	
AND GIRLS	Saunders
DOG TRAINING FOR KIDS	Benjamin
DOG TRAINING, Koehler Method of	Koehler
GO FIND! Training Your Dog to Track	Davis
GUARD DOG TRAINING, Koehler Method of	
Koehler	
OPEN OBEDIENCE FOR RING, HOME	
AND FIELD, Koehler Method of	Koehler
SPANIELS FOR SPORT (English)	Radcliffe
SUCCESSFUL DOG TRAINING, The	
Pearsall Guide to	Pearsall
TRAIN YOUR OWN GUN DOG,	
How to	Goodall
TRAINING THE RETRIEVER	Kersley
TRAINING YOUR DOG TO WIN	
OBEDIENCE TITLES	Morsell
UTILITY DOG TRAINING, Koehler Method of	
Koehler	

Breeding

ART OF BREEDING BETTER DOGS, New	Onstott
HOW TO BREED DOGS	Whitney
HOW PUPPIES ARE BORN	Prine
INHERITANCE OF COAT COLOR	
IN DOGS	Little

General

COMPLETE DOG BOOK, The	
	Official Pub. of American Kennel Club
DISNEY ANIMALS, World of	Koehler
DOG IN ACTION, The	Lyon
DOG BEHAVIOR, New Knowledge of	
Pfaffenberger	
DOG JUDGING, Nicholas Guide to	Nicholas
DOG NUTRITION, Collins Guide to	Collins
DOG PEOPLE ARE CRAZY	Riddle
DOG PSYCHOLOGY	Whitney
DOG STANDARDS ILLUSTRATED	
DOGSTEPS, Illustrated Gait at a Glance	Elliott
ENCYCLOPEDIA OF DOGS, International	
Dangerfield, Howell & Riddle	
JUNIOR SHOWMANSHIP HANDBOOK	
Brown & Mason	
MY TIMES WITH DOGS	Fletcher
RICHES TO BITCHES	Shattuck
SUCCESSFUL DOG SHOWING, Forsyth Guide to	
Forsyth	
TRIM, GROOM AND SHOW YOUR DOG,	
How to	Saunders
WHY DOES YOUR DOG DO THAT?	Bergman
WILD DOGS in Life and Legend	Riddle
WORLD OF SLED DOGS, From Siberia to	
Sport Racing	Coppinger
OUR PUPPY'S BABY BOOK (blue or pink)	